Jacqueline Middleton lives in Norwich and is the
Employment Law Advisor and Industrial Tribunal
Representative at the Citizens' Advice Bureau. She is the
Bureaux tutor on employment law for the East Anglia
area, training new volunteers, and is an advisor to other
Citizens' Advice Bureaux for Eastern England. Jacqueline
Middleton also lectures to sixth forms and employers'
associations.

When she is not working or doing research, Jacqueline
Middleton enjoys keeping nature at bay in her garden.

# YOUR RIGHTS AT WORK

## JACQUELINE MIDDLETON

An OPTIMA book

© Jacqueline Middleton 1990

First published in 1990 by
Macdonald Optima, a division of
Macdonald & Co. (Publishers) Ltd

A member of Maxwell Macmillan Pergamon Publishing Corporation

British Library Cataloguing in Publication Data
Middleton, Jacqueline
    Your rights at work.
    1. Great Britain. Employment. Law
    I. Title
    344.104′1125

    ISBN 0-356-15990-6

Macdonald & Co. (Publishers) Ltd
Orbit House
1 New Fetter Lane
London EC4A 1AR

Photoset in 11pt Century Schoolbook by Leaper & Gard Ltd, Bristol, England

Printed and bound in Great Britain by
The Guernsey Press Co. Ltd., Guernsey, Channel Islands.

# CONTENTS

INTRODUCTION     ix

1. WHAT IS A CONTRACT OF EMPLOYMENT?     1
    The relationship between you and your
       employer     2
    The kind of contract – employed/self-employed     2
    Your contract, and how it is made     4
    The way a contract works     6

2. ARRANGING THE CONTRACT WITH YOUR
    EMPLOYER     7
    Questions you might ask at your interview     8
    Wages councils and the Agricultural Wages
       Board     18
    Custom and practice – how your contract
       changes     18

3. TERMINATION AND NOTICE     21
    Termination     21
    Notice     22
    State benefits when your contract is
       terminated     28

4. THE LAW AND YOUR CONTRACT OF
    EMPLOYMENT     30
    Time limits for making your claim     31
    The Employment Protection (Consolidation)
       Act 1978     31
    The Equal Pay Act 1970     33
    The Sex Discrimination Act 1975     37
    The Race Relations Act 1976     39
    The Health and Safety At Work Act 1974     43
    Trade union law     45
    The Wages Act 1986     46

5. SOME OF YOUR BASIC STATUTORY RIGHTS 48
Rights from the commencement of your
employment 49
When you have been working for one month 53
After 13 weeks in your job 54
After working for 26 weeks 56

6. YOUR RIGHTS AFTER TWO YEARS IN
THE SAME EMPLOYMENT 59
Do you qualify? 59
The right not to be unfairly dismissed 61
The right to a redundancy payment 63
Your rights during lay-off or short-time
working 63
Guarantee payments 64
Maternity rights 65
Your rights when there is a takeover or sale
of the business 65

7. DISMISSAL – FAIR OR UNFAIR? 71
When were you dismissed? 71
Dismissals that are fair 72
Dismissals which might be unfair 77

8. REDUNDANCY – AN EXPLANATION 89
Calculating statutory redundancy payment 90
Do you qualify? 90
People who do not qualify for redundancy
payment 91
If you are not paid your redundancy payment 91
What is a redundancy? 92
Selection for redundancy 93
Redundancy – a dismissal 94
Consultation 95
Looking for a new job 95
Alternative employment 97
When the business is sold – transfer of
undertakings 98
When your employer closes the business or
goes bankrupt 99
Death of employer or employee 101

9. LAY-OFF AND SHORT-TIME WORKING          102
   What are lay-offs and short-time working?   102
   Redundancy payments as a result of lay-off
      or short-time                            104
   Guarantee payments                          107

10. RIGHTS WHEN YOU ARE EXPECTING
    A BABY, AND AFTER                          111
    Time off for antenatal care                112
    Illness when you are pregnant              113
    Hazards at work when you are pregnant      113
    Dismissal because of pregnancy             114
    Sex discrimination and pregnancy           115
    Reduction in working hours because of
       pregnancy                               116
    The right to return to work after having a
       baby                                    117
    Maternity leave                            120
    Payments during maternity leave            121
    Conclusion                                 126

11. INDUSTRIAL TRIBUNALS AND HOW
    THEY WORK                                  127
    Legal aid for representation at Tribunal   128
    Deciding to take your case to a Tribunal   128
    Time limits                                129
    The grievance procedure – have you used it?  131
    Making a claim to an Industrial Tribunal   132
    ACAS – what they do and how they can help  135

12. THE ACTUAL TRIBUNAL                        136
    Who sits on Industrial Tribunals ?         136
    What happens at a Tribunal?                136
    The decision                               137
    Costs and expenses                         139
    Appealing against the decision of an Industrial
       Tribunal                                140

    USEFUL ADDRESSES                           141

# CONTENTS

FURTHER READING               145

SPECIMEN FORMS               147

INDEX                        163

# INTRODUCTION

There are many fixed ideas about people's 'rights' in their employment, and although some of these beliefs are correct the field of employment law changes so often that it is almost impossible for the average person to keep up with it all.

When using this book it will be helpful to read the initial chapters on contract and notice (Chapters 1, 2 and 3) before going on to any specific problem. This will set the scene for understanding the make-up of an employment contract and how the various laws affect it during the course of time. The most important thing to remember is that situations where a possible case can be taken to an Industrial Tribunal carry a time limit, so any decision to complain must be made as soon as possible after the problem arises (see table on page 130).

A book of this size can in no way cover all aspects of the rules governing employees' rights, or the complex decisions required to be made when trouble is encountered in the workplace – it can only serve as a guide or outline to alert the person concerned. The language of the law and lawyers is interpreted and the Acts of Parliament explained, so that the person reading it can decide whether to proceed further into the possibility of being able to enforce their rights in Tribunal or court.

Good industrial relations are based on communication between the employer and employee at all levels. In every case attention should be drawn to the need for discussion or negotiation before any action is taken as a result of a complaint.

This book does not set out to be an instruction manual for making a case in the Industrial Tribunal. It is only a guide to the situations in which an employee might consider making a complaint. It is constantly stressed that whatever the problem, help and advice should be sought from skilled advisers without delay.

Jacqueline Middleton

The information in this book is correct at the date of going to press.

# 1.
# WHAT IS A CONTRACT OF EMPLOYMENT?

The contract of employment is the arrangement made between a person who wishes to work and the person or company who wants them to do the work. As your contract is made up of various parts, or strands, such as pay, hours, kind of job, etc., perhaps it might be described as an invisible rope stretching between you and your employer which will remain there until one of you decides to cut it and finish the relationship.

**Everyone who is employed by someone else has a contract.** Often people think that they do not have a contract because they do not having anything in writing or they have not signed anything. This is not so. The contract is a verbal agreement between employer and employee and is a firm legal arrangement which, if necessary, can be acted upon in court. In practice there is often a letter from the employer stating such things as starting date, wages and other details about what the employer wants you to do in the job; this amounts to an outline of the contract which can be useful as a guide if there is any argument at a later date.

You are entitled to written terms and conditions of your contract after working for 13 weeks (see Chapter 5, page 54).

## THE RELATIONSHIP BETWEEN YOU AND YOUR EMPLOYER

In order for a contract of employment to work there has to be an employer and an employee, and each side has their own responsibilities to the other.

1   The **employer** gives the orders and says what is to be done in the job, but at the same time they have a duty to take care of the employees and to see that their working conditions are up to standard.
2   On the other hand, the **employee** has to do the work provided for them by the employer and they must be a loyal and trustworthy worker.

Each person involved in the contract of employment should clearly understand what is expected of them and, ideally, these facts should be fully discussed during the initial interview.

## THE KIND OF CONTRACT – EMPLOYED/SELF-EMPLOYED

**If you are to be an employee you will have a contract of service.** This means exactly what it says. Your employer will tell you what they want you to do for them and you will give your service in exchange for their paying you. When a person is employed under a contract of service, usually the employer:

1   Pays their income tax and national insurance contributions.
2   Tells them when and where to work and what holidays and sick pay arrangements are to be made.
3   If there is any problem the employer disciplines them in some way or another.
4   The person has to report for work themself; they cannot engage anyone else to do the work for them.
5   Above all, they cannot be said to be in business for themselves.

In other words they are an **employee**. If, on the other hand, someone:

1 Pays their own income tax and national insurance contributions.
2 They come to work when they choose.
3 If they cannot come to work themself they can employ someone else to take their place.
4 They generally have control of how they work from day to day.

In this case they will be thought to be in business on their own – they are **self-employed**.

There was a recent case of a Mr Robinson who worked for a removals firm. He worked for three days a week driving their van and taking and delivering furniture; he wore the firm's uniform, used the firm's vans and the working hours were arranged and enforced by management. He had to be in at 9 am, work until a certain time each evening and take orders from the foreman. He arranged his holidays at a time that was convenient for the firm, but they did not pay him while he was on holiday. He also paid his own income tax and national insurance contributions. Mr Robinson said that he was self-employed, the firm said that he was self-employed, but at the end of the day the court said that his contract was a contract of service and that he was an employee of the firm. In this case it was shown that, in spite of what both the employer and employee may say and believe, the contract is something on its own as far as the nature of the agreement is concerned once it is set up and working, and will be considered as such by a court or Industrial Tribunal.

In the case of Mr Robinson, although he said that he was self-employed, he had to go to work in person and report in at 9 am on the orders of the firm. He had to drive to wherever he was told, and do whatever tasks the foreman told him to do. He also wore the firm's uniform and used the firm's tools and van during the course of his work. In spite of the fact that he was paying his own tax and was not a part of the firm's pay-as-you-earn (PAYE) arrangements he still could not claim that he was not an employee.

Each employment contract will be different, and each one is considered separately, but Mr Robinson's case gives a general idea of what constitutes a contract of service – employment.

This is a rather grey area, but if you are in any doubt about the status of your contract after looking at it in these ways, your local Inland Revenue office would be able to advise you.

## YOUR CONTRACT, AND HOW IT IS MADE

The contract, like a rope, is made up of numerous strands. There are three main parts which contain other sections, making a complete whole. The various parts of a contract of employment are called the terms and conditions. The three principal terms are:

1 Expressed terms
2 Implied terms
3 Imposed terms

### Expressed terms
These are the arrangements that are talked about at the interview or written about in the letter of acceptance or in any other document which the employer might give the employee. They might be such things as what the job consists of, what the wages are, what the hours of work are to be, etc.

### Implied terms
The implied terms are things that are so obvious that it is usually not thought necessary to say anything about them at the interview or to write them down – such things are

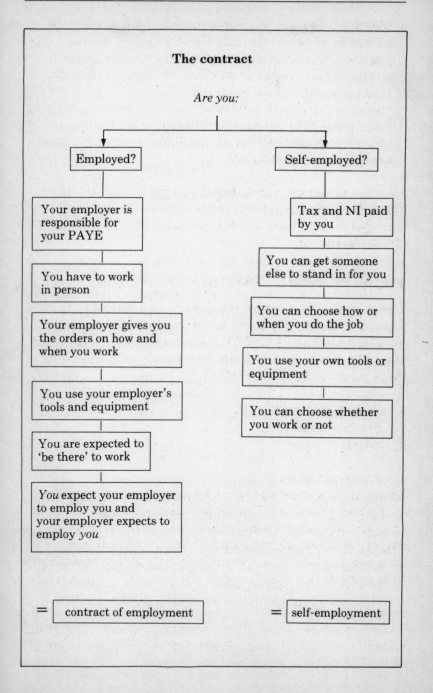

**The contract**

*Are you:*

| Employed? | Self-employed? |
|---|---|
| Your employer is responsible for your PAYE | Tax and NI paid by you |
| You have to work in person | You can get someone else to stand in for you |
| Your employer gives you the orders on how and when you work | You can choose how or when you do the job |
| You use your employer's tools and equipment | You use your own tools or equipment |
| You are expected to 'be there' to work | You can choose whether you work or not |
| *You* expect your employer to employ you and your employer expects to employ *you* | |

= contract of employment

= self-employment

honesty, loyalty, obedience, etc. Although the employee may not have been told in so many words about the existence of certain terms of the contract, it is assumed that they apply and that they have been agreed.

For instance, if something is regularly done in a particular industry it will be assumed that anyone joining that industry will follow suit. An example is the custom of deductions from wages in the weaving industry for bad workmanship, which is generally known or assumed to be known by the weaving trade as a whole. Anyone joining that industry might be said to have this as an implied term of their contract from the start.

### Imposed terms

Imposed terms are terms that are imposed by something outside the employment and outside the contract. Perhaps the most obvious imposed term is that of the need, by law, for a person employed to drive a motor vehicle to hold a current driving licence. These terms are imposed by various laws calculated to ensure that the employee is treated properly, for instance the requirements under the Health and Safety at Work Act to ensure that both employer and employee observe the safety rules at work (see Chapter 4, pages 43–45).

## THE WAY A CONTRACT WORKS

The contract of employment is most important to a worker; whatever the contract says is what the job will be. In law the contract is something on its own, like a rope, which is made up of stated and unstated parts which both the employer and employee believe to be necessary to make the relationship work, and at the end of the day it will be what the contract consists of which will be of the most utmost importance in any claim before a court.

# 2.
# ARRANGING THE CONTRACT WITH YOUR EMPLOYER

A contract of employment is like any other contract between two people in many respects. It is made up of three ingredients:

1  **Offer.** An employer puts an advertisement in the paper, a card in the Jobcentre or shop window, or they put the word round among existing employees, that a job is becoming vacant. This constitutes an offer to the general public (or to other employees) by the employer to set up a contract of employment with another person.

2  **Acceptance.** When you see an advertisement, or hear about a job, you may decide to apply for an interview. At this interview you will discuss the job in detail and may make up your mind to take the position. When you tell the employer that you will take the job, that is the acceptance.

3  **Consideration.** The third part of the contract is the consideration. This is the service and skill which you are giving your employer and the wages which they in their turn will pay you for those services. These are the essential ingredients which hold the contract together, that make it work, that make it a legal relationship.

## QUESTIONS YOU MIGHT ASK AT YOUR INTERVIEW

The interview is very important to your future in a job. It is up to you to find out what you will be expected to do if you are successful in getting the job.

The following are some of the main terms of your contract that you should be told about by an employer. If they do not tell you, then you should ask.

### What kind of job is being offered?

Make sure you know exactly what the job consists of. If there is anything that you think will be difficult for you to do, now is the time to raise it with the employer.

### What is the pay for the job?

Remember that the wages being offered for the job will be subject to deductions for income tax and national insurance, so the pay may appear much higher than the amount that you would actually get.

There is no such thing as a minimum wage, unless the employment is covered by a wages council order (see below) or the rate has been subject to a union agreement, in which case the amount you will be paid will be clearly set out. For other jobs it is a matter to be decided by each individual employer and it will be up to you as the employee to take it or leave it.

While discussing your pay you might ask about bonus payments, and how the wages are to be paid, i.e. weekly, monthly, by cash, cheque, direct payment, etc. Again, this will be a matter for the employer to decide at the beginning of the contract, but they should make it clear to you what the arrangements are. Most wages are paid in arrears, which means that you have to work for a certain time, usually a week (if you are paid weekly) or a month (if you are paid monthly), before you get paid for your work. In some employments you will have to work a week in hand, which means that you have to work a whole week without being paid and then another before you are paid.

The money for your week in hand should then be refunded to you when you leave your employment.

## What are the basic hours and overtime?

The hours that you will be expected to work are very important. You should find out about starting times, breaks and finishing times so that you can fall in with the employer's wishes from the start. Time-keeping is a very important part of the contract and an employee who is not a good time-keeper is heading for trouble. You should ask about overtime and if it is paid at a higher rate than the basic hours. If overtime is arranged on a regular basis it can become part of the contract.

The hours to be worked in any employment are contractual, that is to say a matter of arrangement between you and your employer, and may be varied by negotiation and agreement throughout your employment, as the need arises. The exceptions are those employments covered by wages councils, union agreements and the agricultural wages orders. The amount of hours you work can affect your statutory rights (see Chapter 5, page 48).

## What is your holiday entitlement?

Most holidays are a matter of arrangement with your employer. The only general holidays to which you will be entitled are the two public holidays, Christmas Day and Good Friday, and the six bank holidays which occur throughout the year.

Unless your employment is governed by union agreements your holidays will be decided by your employer. There is no general rule as to the amount of holiday that you will have, but nowadays it is usually about four weeks per year in most jobs.

In some jobs it will be the rule that you have to work for a year before you earn any entitlement to holiday of any kind, so you will be taking your holidays in arrears during the second year of your employment.

You can generally only take your holidays in the current holiday year; this may be in the year from

December to December or April to April, whichever your employer takes as his calculation year. If you have not used all your holiday entitlement in any one year, you may actually lose it as it is not usual to be allowed to carry part of a holiday over into the next holiday year.

When you leave your job, if you have not taken all your holiday you should be paid your accrued holiday pay. This means the payment for the holiday time that you have not taken up to the date of your leaving.

*Bank holidays*   Employees are generally entitled to time off for bank holidays, but in many employments it will be usual for people to work on the day and either have time off on another day, in lieu of working, or be paid at the overtime rate for the day.

## What are the notice arrangements?

You should clearly understand at your interview what notice period will apply to the contract when, or if, it is terminated. There are two kinds of notice – statutory and contractual – which are discussed in detail in Chapter 3. It is important that you know and understand what amount of notice you will be entitled to at the end of your employment.

## What are the sick-pay arrangements?

It is to be expected that an employee will fall sick from time to time during the course of their work. Most employers ask that a sick employee contact them or get a message to them as early as possible on the first morning of the sickness. You should always keep in contact with your employer if you are off sick, either by telephone or message, to keep them informed of the progress of your illness. You will also have to send in your sick notes from the doctor if you are sick for longer than seven days.

*Payment from the state while you are off sick*   When you are unable to work because you are sick you may qualify for **statutory sick pay** (SSP). This is payment made to you by your employer after the first three days (known as waiting days) of your absence through sickness. **The first three days of sickness are not paid.**

After the first three days, your employer must pay you SSP, depending on the amount you earn and whether you qualify. SSP is paid by your employer and they claim it back at a later date from the Department of Social Security (DSS). If you think you qualify for SSP you should check the amount with your local DSS or seek help from the Citizens Advice Bureau. Statutory sick pay can continue for a period of up to 28 weeks. If you have two or more periods of sickness, not more than eight weeks apart, they will be counted as one. This means that you will be able to go straight on to SSP when you are sick the second time without losing the three waiting days.

After you have been absent through sickness for seven days you must produce a self-certificate for your employer. This is a form, **SC1** (see specimen forms, pages 153–158), which you get from your local DSS office (they will post it to you) or from your doctor's surgery. You fill it in and give it, or send it, to your employer as soon as possible. If you are sick longer than seven days you will have to ask your doctor to provide a certificate which you must give or send to your employer. If you do not do this you may lose your entitlement to payment for the days on which you have been absent.

*Contractual (or company) sick pay*  Many employers have private sick-pay schemes, usually enabling the employer to top-up an employee's wages. The most common contractual sick-pay scheme will pay you the difference between your statutory sick pay and the weekly wages that you would normally receive if you were not sick. This means that you will not lose out by being off sick. These schemes are usually for a limited period, after which you revert to the state benefit appropriate for you at the time. Because a private sick pay scheme is a contractual right it is a matter between you and your employer. If you know that your employer has a scheme and you are not being paid, you have the right to take him to court to force him to pay, as with any other contractual term. Most employers' private sick-pay schemes run without problems and employees are paid without such trouble.

## What is your pension position?

*The basic state pension*    If you have worked and paid national insurance contributions or been credited for contributions for the greater part of your working life, you will be eligible for a **state retirement pension** when you reach retiring age. If you do not qualify for the full rate pension you get a pension at a reduced rate – check with the DSS. The DSS can give you a **pension forecast**; this may not be correct at the time that you finally retire, but it can give you a reasonable idea of the amount of pension you will receive (see specimen forms, pages 147–152).

You will be treated as retired if:

1   You are not doing any work.
2   You are doing some paid work but the pay for that work is under the figure of allowable earnings (check with the DSS at the time when you are thinking of retirement).
3   You are over the higher age limit, whether you have given up work or not.

A wife claiming on her husband's contribution record will have to make a separate claim and must give notice to the DSS of retirement, even if she does not work outside the home.

If you are a married woman who is working, you must apply for yourself. You may receive a pension based on your husband's contribution record. You should claim your right to a retirement pension before or as soon after retirement as possible, as there is a limit to the amount of back-dated pension that will be paid to you.

It is best for you to establish your right to the state retirement pension in advance, before you reach pensionable age. You use a form supplied by the DSS and at the same time you should inform your employer that you intend to retire so that they can see that the correct contributions have been made for you (see specimen forms, pages 147–152).

After you have made a claim for your pension, whether you make your claim before or after retirement, you will be sent by the DSS all the information about their decision on your claim and how your pension is to be made up. If you have any doubts or difficulties regarding your pension, see the DSS pension section or telephone the Social Security on Freeline 0800 666555.

*State earnings related pension*　The state earnings related pension – SERPS – is a pension that you earn by paying the higher rate of national insurance contributions, and is paid on top of your basic state pension. You will **not be eligible for SERPS** if:

1　You pay the married woman's reduced rate of contribution.
2　You have contracted out of the scheme.
3　You have contracted out of SERPS by paying into a free standing additional voluntary contribution scheme (FSVCA).
4　You are self-employed.

If you are **contracted in** to SERPS you receive SERPS on top of an occupational or personal pension, i.e. you decide to stay with the state system.

You are **contracted out** of SERPS if you may decide to leave the state pension scheme and pay into a personal pension plan of your own or an occupational pension scheme.

*Occupational pension*　An occupational pension is set up by the employer in addition to SERPS, but you have the right to opt out of this pension if you wish.

You can also contract out of SERPS and rely solely on the occupational pension if it is sufficient for your needs, or increase it by making additional voluntary contributions (AVCS).

*Personal pensions*   You can choose either to remain in, or contract out of SERPS and pay into a personal plan scheme. The amount you receive from such a scheme depends on the amount invested and on the way it is invested.

If you are not in an occupational pension scheme you can have more than one personal pension. Such a pension can provide a regular income, a basic pension for your dependents should you die in service, and sometimes a lump sum as well.

If you are thinking of taking out a personal plan pension, or of making any decisions on pension matters you should take advice – pensions are complicated. Each person will have a different set of pension needs. Where there is an occupational pension set up by your employer they usually decide whether you will stay contracted-in or contracted-out, but in the field of personal pensions the choices and decisions are extremely varied. You can get advice from a number of sources such as banks, building societies, insurance companies, etc., but whoever is giving advice of this nature must be authorised under the Financial Services Act.

If, when you start your employment, there is a pension scheme, or a pension scheme for employees is proposed:

1   Find out all you can about the scheme.
2   Find out how it is likely to affect you, either when you retire or if you leave that employment.
3   Get the best possible advice and guidance from an authorised person.

*Self-employed*   If you are self-employed you cannot have SERPS or an occupational pension. If you have made the correct amount of contributions you will be entitled to your basic state pension and any personal pension in which you have invested.

*Leaving your job before your retiring date*   If you leave your job for any reason before your retirement date, special arrangements will be made for your pension. It may be that you will have the option of:

1. A Preserved Pension, frozen until your retirement date.
2. Transfer value to be paid to your next employer or an insurance company which will issue a buying-out policy.
3. A cash refund of the capital sum after you have been bought back into SERPS through a payment to the DSS by your employer.

Each of these options will depend on what kind of pension arrangements you have decided to adopt in your employment. Get advice.

## Is there a grievance procedure?

If you have a complaint about anything in your working conditions or the way that you are being treated, you should use the grievance procedure. This simply means the way you can complain to your employer.

Mary was employed as a clerical worker, but later was being trained on the VDU. She was perfectly happy to have this extra skill, but her desk backed on to a window, making it difficult for her to see the screen. She asked her supervisor if the desk could be turned round, but this request was refused. Mary can now use the grievance procedure by appealing to the person above her supervisor to have her difficulty resolved. If this does not sort out the problem, then she should appeal to someone higher up, for instance a director.

In this way problems of any kind in your work can be
sorted out. Most large firms have a written grievance
procedure so that you may easily see who to approach
when you have a problem, but many small firms do not
have any formal arrangements. If that is the case you
must approach the person who is higher up, all along the
line until you get to the top. Of course in very small firms
it may be that there will only be the boss in control, in
which case you will have to put your grievance directly to
him. In these circumstances it is up to you to put your
complaint in a reasonable way – without losing your cool –
and discuss it with your employer.

**If you are dismissed from your employment**
Using the grievance procedure when you have been
dismissed is very important, in several ways:

1   You can put your side of the question and may get
    your job back.
2   You will be seen to be a reasonable employee by trying
    to communicate with your employer, which will be
    helpful if you are going to make a claim to an
    Industrial Tribunal for unfair dismissal at a later date
    (see Chapter 11).
3   From the point of view of the DSS (Department of
    Social Security) you will be making an attempt to keep
    yourself in work and so trying to avoid claiming state
    benefits (see Chapter 3, page 28).

On a personal level, of course, you may be able to make
working conditions, etc., more comfortable.

**Is there any disciplinary procedure?**
The way an employer treats their employees when
something goes wrong must be reasonable in all the
circumstances.
    There is no law which says how many warnings, written
or verbal, an employee must be given, but if an employer
does not give sufficient warning to an employee that their

job is in danger, then they will be judged to have behaved unreasonably. If there are written disciplinary procedures, or there are disciplinary rules, produced by an employer then they must follow them. If they do not do so, any dismissal which occurs will be unfair. If there are no written procedures the position is less clear.

The conciliation service ACAS (Advisory, Conciliation, Arbitration Service) have produced a code of practice which sets out the correct way to discipline an employee who falls out of line. Although this code is not law, it is always taken into consideration as a guideline when an Industrial Tribunal is looking at the way someone has been dismissed.

*Warnings* You might expect to receive, for example, two verbal warnings followed by a final written warning before you are dismissed, or one verbal followed by two written warnings might be reasonable. Warnings should be exactly what they say – they should warn you that you are doing something which your employer considers to be wrong. It might be that you are not doing your work properly, in which case you might be given a warning that if you do not improve, other disciplinary action may be expected; if you continue to do the same thing you must expect further disciplinary measures.

A warning should be made absolutely clear to the employee. Often there is confusion about warnings. The employer may give the employee a telling-off, and, at a later date, claim that there was a verbal warning. If you are doing something wrong and you receive a serious reprimand from your employer (or a senior member of staff) you would do well to ask if this is meant as a formal warning. In many cases an employee is given a letter confirming a verbal warning, which makes the position more clear.

A warning is not in itself a sanction. It is meant to help the employee to improve, and for the employment to run more smoothly.

*Gross misconduct*   If you do something that amounts to gross industrial misconduct then you must expect to be dismissed without a warning of any kind. Some things that might amount to gross misconduct are theft, fighting, disobeying a lawful order from your superior, negligence, etc., and there are of course many more.

## WAGES COUNCILS AND THE AGRICULTURAL WAGES BOARD

Certain industries are covered by wages councils, which control things like working conditions, meal breaks, wages, etc. The councils themselves are made up of a number of employers and an equal number of trade union representatives, and there are different councils for different industries.

The wages councils are gradually being reduced, and it is thought that they may eventually disappear completely. At the moment, though, they control several industries such as clothing manufacturing, hairdressing, the retail trades (food and non-food) and the catering trade. Agricultural workers have their own board which controls them in the same way as the wages councils control other industries.

If an industry is covered by a wages council there should be a list of current rates of pay, etc., displayed where all the staff can see it. Lists of employments currently covered by wages councils are to be found at Citizens Advice Bureaux and at your local Jobcentre. If you think that your job is covered by an order, and you have a problem, you can get in touch with your nearest wages inspectorate (addresses on page 141) for help.

## CUSTOM AND PRACTICE – HOW YOUR CONTRACT CHANGES

When you start your job you will have sorted out all the above terms and conditions, as arranged with your employer. Again, taking the idea of an invisible rope

## The terms of your contract

*In summary, things you should be asking at your job interview:*

Pay
▶
> How much is the pay?
> How will you be paid, and how often?
> (weekly/monthly)

Holidays
▶
> How much paid holiday will you get?

Hours
▶
> What are the hours you will be expected to work, and how many per week?

Notice
▶
> What notice will you be given if you have to leave – and what notice will you be expected to give and is it more than the statutory notice?

Sickness
▶
> What will you have to do if you are sick, and will you be paid by your employer?

Pension
▶
> Does the firm have a pension scheme?

Disciplinary rules
▶
> What will happen if you do something wrong or you are to be dismissed?

Grievance procedures
▶
> How can you appeal if you think things are not right at your work or if you are given a warning, or are dismissed?

between you and your employer, the contract, like a rope, will be made up of all the strands or terms to which you have agreed; however, with the passing of time those strands may alter and change.

For instance, you may have agreed to start your work at 9 am, but after a while you realise that your bus gets in at 8.55 am which makes it difficult for you to be ready to work at 9 am. If it is convenient for your employer, they may agree that you can start at 9.15 am – and so it becomes part of your contract that your starting time is 9.15 am. Of course, they may say that you will have to catch an earlier bus.

Sometimes things in a job change without there being any particular discussion about it – people just start doing things differently or new orders are given from time to time. This changes the contract, or parts of it, and is known as custom and practice; in other words, it is the custom that something is done in a certain way.

When you have sorted out the above terms and conditions of your job you will have a fair idea of what is expected of you and what you may expect from your employer, and you will be ready to start in your new job.

# 3.
# TERMINATION
# AND NOTICE

## TERMINATION

When a contract of employment comes to an end it is said
to have been terminated. There are several ways in which
your contract can be terminated.

### Termination by agreement

Sometimes a contract of employment comes to an end
when both the employer and employee decide that it is
time to part. They both agreed to the start of the
employment and they have both agreed to the ending. It
may be on any terms that they both agree; for instance,
they may both agree that they will waive any period of
notice or that a period of notice may be longer or shorter
to suit the situation. In this case the employee may resign
or the employer give notice and there will be no dispute.

### Expiry of a fixed term contract

A fixed term contract is one that has been arranged to end
on a particular date. The date on which it is to end is
arranged – fixed – at the start of the contract and it
terminates on that date.

Some contracts of this kind depend on funds being
available for them to keep going; if the funds run out, the
contract terminates at that time. Rather less often
someone is taken on to do a particular job or fulfill a
specific task; when that job or task is completed the
contract is said to have terminated.

### By operation of law the contract disappears

Your contract can come to an end if you are away from

work due to long-term sickness, or if you are serving a sentence in prison.

An accident can bring the contract to an end, particularly if you are unable to continue doing your job owing to the injuries you sustained. In order for it to be said that the contract is terminated it is necessary to look at all the circumstances at the time, such as how long you have been away from work, when your medical advisers think you will be able to return or whether you will recover enough to continue with your job. For instance, if you have injured your back it will be unlikely that you will be able to go back to heavy labouring or unloading lorries.

**Termination by breach**
This means that the contract is ended by a definite action on the part of the employer or the employee. For example, the employer dismisses the employee for bad conduct or absenteeism, or the employee resigns because of the employer's behaviour or the way they are being treated.

**Summary dismissal**
When are you summarily dismissed the contract is terminated immediately because of your gross industrial misconduct – conduct on your part which is extremely serious and which your employer is entitled to say breaks the relationship between you. In these circumstances he can tell you that you must leave immediately and your contract will be at an end. The kind of conduct meriting summary dismissal might be fighting, stealing, disobeying an order from a superior or breaking a health and safety rule.

NOTICE

When your employer intends to dismiss you (i.e. your contract is terminated) he must give you warning that this is going to happen. This warning time is called notice. You will, in most circumstances, be entitled to notice from your employer. And you will also be expected to give notice to your employer if it is you that wishes to leave your job.

Like any other term of your contract, notice from you or your employer **does not have to be written** down; you can simply say 'I want to leave and I am giving you my notice' for it to become a fact. However in practice an employer usually says, for example, 'I am going to dismiss you' and then confirms that fact by letter. It is much more satisfactory if it is put into writing at the time as then there will be no dispute and it will be helpful for the DSS when you apply for benefits (see below).

The fact that notice can be verbal does not affect your employer's legal obligation to supply you with written reasons for your dismissal in most circumstances (see Chapter 5).

There are two kinds of notice:

1   Statutory.
2   Contractual.

**Statutory notice**
Statutory notice is the notice that has to be given by law.

The law governing employment contracts says that in the normal way everyone is entitled to a certain amount of notice that their contract is going to be terminated, for whatever reason. The length of notice that must be given by an employer to an employee is clearly set out, and depends on the length of service in complete years that you have worked for the same (or an associated) employer.

> Mary Fisher has worked for the Happy Dye Co. Ltd for three years and ten months. She is being dismissed because she is continually clocking in late. She will be entitled to three weeks' statutory notice.

The statutory notice required from an employer to an employee is as follows:

1 No notice if the employee has worked for less than one month.
2 One week's notice if the employee has worked over one month but less than two years.
3 One week's notice for every year of service, up to a maximum of 12 weeks.

Fred Johns has been a warehouseman for 16 years. He can no longer lift the crates to load lorries, so his employer is dismissing him. He will get 12 weeks statutory notice.

You, as an employee, must give your employer one week's statutory notice, no matter how long you have worked for him.

## Contractual notice

The second kind of notice is contractual – it is part of an arrangement made between you and your employer and it is a term of your contract.

Your employer cannot say that he will give you less than the minimum statutory notice, but he can say that you will be entitled to more. Contractual notice is agreed at the time of setting up the contract and, like any other term, can be a verbal undertaking. It is often the case that contractual notice is for a fixed amount such as a month, and often the arrangement will be a month's notice on either side. If this is what is suggested as part of your contract when you want to leave you will have to give your employer that amount of notice.

If either side (you or your employer) do not give proper notice they are said to have breached the contract, and they could be sued for damages in the county court. This means that by not giving notice they have broken their part of the agreement; therefore they are in the wrong, and they may have to pay for it.

So, if you want to leave your job make sure that you give your employer proper notice, and if you are dismissed by your employer make sure that you have been given the

## Notice – what is your entitlement?

1   If you have worked over four weeks, you will be entitled to *statutory* notice under your contract.

2   You may have an arrangement with your employer for a set amount of notice which will be *contractual* notice.
    (Contractual notice cannot be *less* than statutory notice.)

3   If your contract comes to an end, the law says you will be entitled to:

> *either* statutory notice *or* contractual notice
> *whichever is the longer.*

*Examples*

A   If you have worked for the same employer for *two years* and are dismissed:

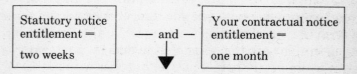

| Statutory notice entitlement = | | Your contractual notice entitlement = |
|---|---|---|
| two weeks | — and — | one month |

The notice you should be given will be:

> *one month – as in your contract*

You would have to give your employer one month's notice if you wanted to leave as it is *your* part of the contract.

B   If you have worked under the same contract for *six years* and are dismissed:

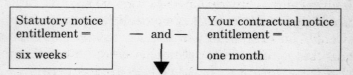

| Statutory notice entitlement = | | Your contractual notice entitlement = |
|---|---|---|
| six weeks | — and — | one month |

The notice you should be given will be:

> *six weeks – which is the statutory notice*

correct amount of notice. You will be entitled to the amount of statutory notice or the amount of contractual notice, whichever is the longer.

## Working out your notice

If your employer has given you notice it may be that you will be required to go on working under notice until your termination date, when you stop working.

For example, if you have worked for the same employer (or an associated company) for three full years and you are given notice, you should be given that notice three weeks before the date you will leave. During that time you will continue to work under your contract in the normal way, with the employer paying you wages and making all the usual deductions for income tax and national insurance, until the last day you work.

## Not working out your notice (money in lieu)

Often an employer who intends to dismiss a person does not wish them to continue working while they are under notice. In this case the employee should be given what is known as money in lieu of notice; in other words, the employer has to pay an amount equal to the weeks of notice-time which he should have given. Money in lieu of notice simply means money instead of notice.

For example, if you have worked for the same employer (or associate company) for three full years, and your employer dismisses you without giving you notice, he must pay you three weeks' wages in lieu, or instead of, that notice.

Wages paid in lieu of notice are paid gross, i.e. the employer does not have to deduct amounts for tax or national insurance from the amount he pays you in lieu of notice. So you may want to make a voluntary payment to the DSS to maintain your national insurance contribution record for certain state benefits such as your pension. For example, if you are given 12 weeks' money in lieu of notice, there will be a 12-week gap in your contribution record, which could reduce your entitlement to such things as unemployment benefit later on. Get advice from your local DSS office about how to find out about your contribution position.

## Given notice and not required to work

Sometimes an employer who has dismissed an employee will take the view that it is better that they do not go on working as usual during their notice period. In many cases this can make sense from the employer's point of view as an employee who is under notice can make trouble with other staff or upset customers and associates.

The employer can pay money in lieu of notice and finish the employee's contract there and then, but it may be that he prefers not to lay out what might be a considerable sum in one go. The alternative is to say to the employee 'You are under notice, but you are not required to work during that notice period. You will be paid as normal (by the week or by the month) until the termination date.' In that case you would be paid exactly as usual, with deductions for tax and national insurance, but you would not have to work.

Sometimes an employer will ask that you take any holiday owing to you in that period.

## When you might be dismissed without notice

Dismissal without notice can occur when an employee is instantly, or summarily, dismissed.

An employer can dismiss you instantly if you commit an act of gross industrial misconduct such as theft, fighting, fraud, etc. (see Chapter 2, page 18). The employer is entitled to tell you to leave the premises immediately and no notice or payment of any kind will be owing to you because you will have broken your contract by your behaviour. You must, of course, be paid for any work you have done up to the time of your dismissal, but no notice or notice money will be paid.

If you believe that you have been unfairly dismissed it may be that the notice money could form part of any compensation figure paid to you after an Industrial Tribunal decision (see Chapter 12).

## Notice you must give your employer

If you have worked for an employer for over one month and you decide that you want to leave in the ordinary way, you must give **one week's notice** to your employer.

Your notice does not have to be in writing; you can simply tell him that you wish to leave and that you will be finishing on a particular date in a week's time. If you do this, you will continue to work out your notice and be paid in the usual way up to the last day that you work.

If it is part of your contract that you must give a certain amount of notice to your employer when you leave, for example one month's notice, then you will have to give this amount, although it is of course longer than the minimum statutory notice. If you leave your employment without giving your employer the correct amount of notice he or she could sue you for breach of contract. It is best to attempt to negotiate with your employer in these circumstances and try to avoid bad feelings.

## STATE BENEFITS WHEN YOUR CONTRACT IS TERMINATED

When your contract has come to an end you may be entitled to *unemployment benefit*. Whether or not you will get unemployment benefit depends on:

1   Your national insurance contribution record.
    **or**
2   The reason for leaving your employment.

At the end of your employment you should go and sign on at your local unemployment office. You will be given a form to fill in and the DSS will look into your record. If you have made enough national insurance contributions you will receive payment of unemployment benefit. If you do not qualify for this benefit, it may be that you will be entitled to other state benefits; you should ask the DSS for further information.

## Unemployment benefit disallowed

If, when you have signed on, the DSS adjudication officer decides that they need more information about the circumstances of your leaving, they may suspend payment of your unemployment benefit until they have made further investigations and they are satisfied that you qualify. After full enquiries of you and your ex-employer they may decide that you left your job and became unemployed without good reason, or that you caused your own dismissal by misconduct, in which case you will be deemed to have made yourself voluntarily unemployed and your benefit may be suspended or disallowed.

You can appeal against this decision of the adjudication officer to a social security appeals tribunal (SSAT). You have **three months** from the date upon which your benefit was suspended in which to lodge your appeal. If you need help with preparing an appeal to the SSAT you can get advice from your local Citizens Advice Bureau, Law Centre, etc.

# 4.
# THE LAW AND YOUR CONTRACT OF EMPLOYMENT

The first thing to remember is that everyone who works for an employer has a contract of employment.

When you are in work, you will be covered, or protected, by various laws which are known as Acts. These are Acts of Parliament which have been developed over the years to suit the needs of people in work and the people who employ them. The law itself is never static, and the way it is interpreted is always changing.

The original Acts themselves are amended and added to from time to time as Parliament thinks fit, by Statutory Instruments. The Acts are also affected by European law, European regulations being added to standing Acts of Parliament by way of Directives.

Some of the Acts which cover employment do not protect everyone, and some require you to have worked certain lengths of time before you come under their protection. Others apply to everyone from the first day that they are employed simply because they are an employee (see table on page 58). In every case, if you think that you may have a claim against your employer, you will need to get advice from someone knowledgeable as soon as possible. If you are a member of a trade union you should ask your union representative to help you. You may find that you need to contact your local branch office of your union to give you this kind of advice. If you do not belong to a union, you can get advice from your local Law

Centre, if you have one, or from the Citizens Advice Bureau.

If it turns out that you have a possible case against your employer you can make a claim for your rights under the appropriate Act or Acts. The Department of Employment issues leaflets on your rights, which are kept in Jobcentres, unemployment benefit offices and Citizens Advice Bureaux.

## TIME LIMITS FOR MAKING YOUR CLAIM

Most of your statutory rights under Acts of Parliament carry a time limit for entering a claim to the Industrial Tribunal (see table on page 130). These time limits are very strict; hence the need to get advice and act quickly. If you do not get your initial claim to the Tribunal office in time, the Tribunal may have to say that they have no jurisdiction to hear the case. This means that they are not allowed, under law, to hear your case because you have been late with your claim.

In most cases an application presented out of time is not heard by the Tribunal.

## THE EMPLOYMENT PROTECTION (CONSOLIDATION) ACT 1978

This is the Act which is concerned with all aspects of employment. The EP(C)A, as it is known, is the Act which includes laws relating to the contract, redundancy, trade union activities and things like maternity rights and how you will be paid if your employer is insolvent. This Act has been updated from time to time by amendments which have either changed parts of it or added to it. It is also influenced by European law which brings our law into line with Europe; the European laws come to us in the form of Regulations or Articles which are added to our Acts of Parliament. At the time of writing (November 1989) there are certain changes to be made to some parts of the Act in the form of a Bill, which will soon become law. The proposed changes are listed and explained in the following chapters as and when they apply.

Subject to certain qualifications and exceptions (see Chapter 6) the EP(C)A 1978 relates to all employees who have a contract for:

1   Work of over 16 hours per week.
    **or**
2   Between 8 hours and 16 hours if you have worked for the same employer (or an associated employer) for over 5 years.

Most of the claims made by employees under this Act will be heard in an **Industrial Tribunal**, a type of court set up to deal with problems in employment (see Chapter 11).

Some of the rights you may have under the EP(C)A 1978 include the right to:

1   An itemised pay statement showing deductions from wages.
2   Time off from work for antenatal care.
3   Time off from work for public or trade union duties.
4   A minimum period of notice.
5   A written statement of the terms and conditions of employment.
6   Not to be prevented from becoming a member of a recognised trade union.
7   Maternity pay, and the right to return to work after having a baby.
8   The right not to be unfairly dismissed.
9   A written statement giving reasons for dismissal.
10  A redundancy payment.
11  Redundancy payment after a period of lay-off or short-time.
12  Redundancy payment and money in lieu of notice, etc., when your employer is insolvent.
13  If the business is sold, the right for your contract of employment to be transferred to the new owner.
14  The right to make a claim to an Industrial Tribunal on any of the above issues.

As this is the main Act covering employment, it will be dealt with in some detail in the chapters which follow. Your rights – and the laws giving them to you as an employee, and how you can enforce them – are laid out and explained.

## THE EQUAL PAY ACT 1970

The Equal Pay Act was put on the statute book in 1970, but it was not until December 1975 that it came into force, along with the Sex Discrimination Act (see page 37). At this time the Equal Opportunities Commission was established and empowered to look after the running of the two Acts.

The **Equal Opportunities Commission** can help you proceed with a claim under either of the Acts. The EOC issue very helpful booklets on the subject of discrimination in all its aspects. These booklets may be obtained from Jobcentres, some Citizens Advice Bureaux or direct from the EOC in Manchester (see addresses, page 141).

Sometimes it is difficult to decide whether your claim falls under the Sex Discrimination Act or the Equal Pay Act. For instance, if you are a woman and you are being paid less money than a man for the same job, then your claim will be under the Equal Pay Act, but if your complaint concerns the offer of a job then it will fall under the Sex Discrimination Act.

A man who is treated less favourably than a woman in his work can use the Act to make a complaint to an Industrial Tribunal, although the majority of cases are still those of women bringing complaints. The basic idea of the Equal Pay Act is that built into the contract of employment is an equality clause; this means that all employees are promised equal treatment in the same employment where there is:

1   Work which is **like** work.
    **or**

2  Work which has been **rated as equivalent**.
   **or**
3  Work which is of **equal value**.

A woman who was employed as a waitress was doing exactly the same kind of work as the only male waiter, but being paid 12p per hour less than him. This lady did not realise that she could complain of this treatment until after the man had been promoted to banqueting supervisor, but it was found that the equality clause in her contract had been in operation while the two of them had been working side by side, and therefore she was entitled to the same rate as the man before his promotion.

## Like work or work of a broadly similar nature
The Act says that people should receive the same pay for the same work, without discrimination on the grounds of sex. It is the kind of work actually done which will count, not what is supposed to be done under the contract.

Mrs Brodie was a driller. She claimed that she should be paid the same as a male driller who got 30p per hour more than her. But the man provided his own drill and jig, set his own machine and sharpened and replaced his own drills. In Mrs Brodie's case a chargehand did all these things for her, so it was said that there was a substantial difference in the two jobs of driller and that the two people did not do like work.

In another case two canteen ladies who worked day and noon shifts claimed the same basic pay as a man who worked on permanent night shift in the canteen. The only difference between them was that the women took the food to the tables at breakfast time and the man did not. It was found that this was like work and the ladies succeeded.

## Equivalently rated work
Work which is rated as of equivalent value is work that has been the subject of a **job evaluation study** (JES).

This is a careful assessment of the responsibilities and tasks involved in the performance of a particular person's job, carried out by one of a number of impartial companies who specialise in this field. If a job evaluation study shows that two people are doing equally rated work, then those two people should be treated (and paid) in the same manner.

A JES must be accepted by both the employer and employee if it is to be valid. If the employees do not accept the study and they do not cooperate in its make-up, it may be deemed that the JES itself will be discriminatory.

## Work of equal value

The third and final way in which someone can establish their claim to equal pay under the Equal Pay Act is by showing that their work is of equal value to that of someone of the opposite sex in the same employment. Unfortunately this aspect of the Act and the means of making a claim are extremely complicated – 'more like income tax than a human rights code' was the comment of one of our leading lawyers.

The question of work of equal value is again to be decided on the findings of a job evaluation study, but in this case the work does not have to be of the same kind; for instance, a clerical supervisor has been compared to a computer programmer, and a female cook to a male painter. These jobs cannot, in the ordinary sense, be compared, but under a job evaluation study they may be found to be of equal value. The JES will cover all terms of the contract and therefore things included as well as pay will count towards the final evaluation of the job.

## Making a claim

If you think that you may have a claim under any of the headings in the Equal Pay Act you may make a claim to an Industrial Tribunal at any time during your employment or up to six months after the date on which you were last employed in that job. You may be able to claim arrears of pay for up to two years before the date on which you make your claim, or damages for not receiving non-cash benefits (such as the use of a company car or working clothes, etc.) for the same period. The procedure involved in making a claim is complicated and you should seek advice right from the start.

## People covered by the Act

The Act applies to employees of all ages throughout Great Britain. It applies whether you are working full-time, part-time, or even if you have just started work or have only been at work for a short time, but you must be an employee working under a contract of service or of apprenticeship or be contracted personally to do work. The Act does not normally cover people who work outside Great Britain, but if you are employed in United Kingdom territorial waters (such as an oil or gas installation) or on a ship registered in Great Britain (unless you work wholly outside Great Britain) you will be covered.

The Act covers all matters to do with the employee's contract and all provisions of a collective agreement (see trade union law, page 45).

## Who is not covered?

The Act has certain exceptions:

1   The Act does not let men claim the special treatment afforded to women in matters to do with maternity and childbirth.
2   Nor is equal treatment between men and women required as regards retirement, whether voluntary or not, on grounds of age, length of service, or incapacity, with the exception of people who are members of an occupational pension scheme. Where a man is a member of an occupational pension scheme, then women must also be given the opportunity to become members of such a scheme.
3   The general provisions of the Act do not apply to the armed forces or to the police. They have their own provisions through the Central Arbitration Committee,

and the Secretary of State or the Defence Council may seek their advice if the need arises.

## THE SEX DISCRIMINATION ACT 1975

The Sex Discrimination Act does not only apply to employment; it can also cover such things as education, goods, facilities, services and premises. But for the purpose of this book we will look at the way it affects employment. Certain aspects of the Sex Discrimination Act will be affected by the Employment Bill but they refer more to the way the Act is to be applied than to the Act as described in this book.

The object of the Sex Discrimination Act is to do away with discrimination in employment on the grounds of sex or marital status. Men as well as women are covered by the Act, although the actual wording of the Act is from the woman's angle. The idea is to even up the treatment of employees by making sure that one does not receive **less favourable treatment** than another because of their sex or because they are married.

The Sex Discrimination Act can affect employment from the time a job is advertised or offered. A job offered exclusively to men (or women) may be discriminatory if it is exclusive simply because of sex; for instance, an advertisement for male bar staff or women shop assistants is discriminatory.

## Direct discrimination

It does not matter whether the employer intends to discriminate against someone; it is simply a matter of whether the employer actually treats them differently.

Making women employees wear skirts, and not trousers, when working where the public could see them was said not to be discriminatory because the male employees also had restrictions on what they could wear in the same situation.

## Indirect discrimination

Indirect discrimination by an employer is rather less obvious. For example, an employer is said to have discriminated against women when he applies a requirement or condition to a job which he applies equally to men and women, but which is more difficult for women to comply with.

An employer who says that he will pay full-time workers at a higher rate of pay than that of part-time workers is guilty of indirect discriminations. The argument here is that a considerably smaller number of women will be able to take a full-time job than men, so they will be less favourably treated.

## Discrimination against married persons

Your employer must not treat you differently from other employees because you are married; for instance, an employer must not refuse a woman employment because she has a husband at home to support her, or specifically select her for redundancy for the same reason.

## Victimisation

You may be victimised by being treated differently from your fellow workers because you have brought an equal pay claim against your employer. This victimisation may take the form of your pay being reduced, or your being selected for redundancy. This in itself may constitute sex discrimination under the Sex Discrimination Act.

## If your employer's treatment of you is discriminatory

You may be able to make a complaint to an industrial tribunal. If you think you have a case of sex discrimination you should write to the Equal Opportunities Commission for help or advice. They may provide representation for you at the Industrial Tribunal, or at a higher court if that is necessary. Any claim must be presented within three months from the date upon which the discrimination took place.

THE LAW AND YOUR CONTRACT

## Exceptions in the Sex Discrimination Act

There are certain circumstances in which it is not possible to claim under the Sex Discrimination Act, such as:

1   Smaller employers with five or fewer employees. In looking at how many people are employed you must include any associated employer and treat them as one company. Sometimes your managing director is himself employed by the company, in which case he must be counted.
2   Private households employing housekeepers, maids, butlers, gardeners, etc., for the purposes of a private household.
3   Partnerships with fewer than five partners.

There are also certain situations which are excluded from the Act, such as someone working wholly outside Great Britain. However, if you are working on the continental shelf, i.e. on an offshore oil or gas rig, you will be covered by the Act.

## THE RACE RELATIONS ACT 1976

The Race Relations Act (RRA) enables people to bring claims of racial discrimination directly to the courts and Industrial Tribunals. It extends the idea of what unlawful racial discrimination is, in very much the same way as the Sex Discrimination Act, and, like the Sex Discrimination Act, it covers aspects other than employment for the purposes of discrimination.

The Commission for Racial Equality assists people in their claims, and a special responsibility is placed on local authorities to promote equality of opportunity. The Commission has issued a code of practice to guide people in matters of racial harmony, giving practical advice to employers, employees, unions and employment agencies on how best to eradicate racial discrimination and to help towards equality of opportunity.

## Explanation of terms

*Racial grounds*   The meaning of the words 'on racial grounds' for a claim of racial discrimination is colour, race, nationality or ethnic or national origins. National origins is taken to mean race rather than citizenship. Ethnic origins, on the other hand, can include such people as Sikhs, Jews, etc., who are defined as having common ethnic origins and therefore are a racial group.

*Racial group*   A racial group is similar to racial grounds. The definition of a racial group must be taken in a broad, cultural and historical sense. In fact every one belongs to a racial group of some kind – English, Welsh, Rastafarian, Sikh, Jew, etc. So a racial group could be subdivided into smaller groups; eastern European could include Poles, Slovaks, Hungarians and so on, all living in a different way and speaking different languages, but being part of one racial group. Language is only one of the factors to be considered if you are looking at a possible racial discrimination.

*Racial discimination*   As in the Sex Discrimination Act, discrimination can be either racial discrimination or victimisation. When a person discriminates against another person they treat them less favourably because of their race.

## Direct discrimination
You are being discriminated against if your employer treats you differently because of your race. It does not matter that his treatment of you is only partly influenced by your race; if race is the most substantial reason for the difference in treatment, then you may be able to say that there has been racial discrimination against you.

## Comparing like with like
If you are a black person who is being paid less money than your fellow workers who are white, you must look at

the reason why they are being paid more. Are they more qualified than you? Or are they more senior? Or is there some other reason for the difference?

If there are no distinguishing differences then you must ask yourself if they are being paid more because of their race. If this is so, you will be able to claim that your employer is discriminating against you on the grounds of race.

## Racial segregation
Deliberate separation of one group of people from another on the grounds of race or colour can be claimed as discrimination.

## Discrimination by way of victimisation
If your employer treats you less favourably than other people because you have behaved in any of the following ways he will be discriminating against you under the Race Relations Act:

1  If you bring any proceedings under the Race Relations Act.
2  If you give evidence in any proceedings (against your employer or not) under the Race Relations Act.
3  If you ask questions about a possible racial discrimination case.
4  If you accuse anyone of racial discrimination (it must be in good faith).

## Discrimination before your employment begins
When you apply for a job your prospective employer must not discriminate against you by:

1  Restricting his field of choice of employees on racial grounds.
2  He must not offer to pay less to a prospective employee because of their race, colour, etc.
3  He must not operate a colour (or race) bar in any form.

## Exceptions

*Private households*   If you are applying to work in
someone's home they will be entitled to turn down your
application on grounds of race, colour, etc. if they wish.

*Training schemes*   It is lawful for employers to recruit
people on the grounds of race when the purpose is for
them to be trained for a special purpose. For instance, if a
firm is training people to work in a particular country,
they are able to select candidates of the appropriate race
or colour, on the grounds that they will be training them
and sending them back to work in that country.

*Overseas recruitment of seamen*   Employers can practise
discrimination in their choice of people to serve as seamen
if they are actually recruited abroad. They are not
protected even if they are brought back into Great Britain
in order to sign a contract. However they will be protected
if the employment is connected with work on the
continental shelf, such as exploitation of the subsoil or the
seabed.

*Race as a job qualification*   In some cases the job calls for
someone of a particular race or colour, and without such a
person the whole basis of the employment would not exist.
For instance, you would have to be Chinese to be a chef
producing genuine Chinese food in a Chinese restaurant.

## If you think you are being unlawfully
## discriminated against
If you think that the treatment that you are receiving
from another person may be discriminatory under the
Race Relations Act, you may send a list of questions to
that person asking them for their views on the situation.
This can be done by asking your questions on a special
form which you can get from a Jobcentre or direct from
the Commission for Racial Equality. There are time limits
set for the presentation of the questionnaire if it is to be

used later at a hearing of an Industrial Tribunal, and it would be best to get advice and assistance as soon as possible after the date of your complaint. You must make your complaint to the Industrial Tribunal within three months of the act of unlawful discrimination.

If you think that you have been discriminated against on the grounds of race, colour, etc., you can get assistance from the Commission for Racial Equality.

## THE HEALTH AND SAFETY AT WORK ACT 1974

The Health and Safety at Work Act covers health and safety in the workplace.

### People who are covered by the Act

The Act applies to all persons at work, that is employers, employees, people who are self-employed. It also covers the general well-being of members of the public who may be involved or affected by the work activities, such as passersby.

The **exception** is again people who are employed as domestic servants in private households.

### The scope of the Act

The Act not only covers the health and safety of people at work and the general public, but also the keeping and use of dangerous substances. Control is applied wherever dangerous substances are found, even if they are not actually being used in connection with the work.

The Act also covers the emissions of obnoxious or offensive substances which are airborne. This will cover such things as gases and smells from manufacturing processes which may be a danger to your health or cause damage to the environment.

### The duties of an employer

1 Your employer must provide safe working conditions.
2 Your employer must ensure that a safe system of work is the rule.

3   Your employer must regularly monitor the workplace.
4   A regular check must be made on all safety equipment
    such as personal protective equipment.

If you are working for an employer who has **five or more
employees** he should have prepared a written statement
of his general policy on health and safety and the
arrangements he has made in the event of a breach of the
health and safety rules.

## Your duty as an employee

You have a duty, as an employee, to take reasonable care.
This means that you should take care to avoid injury to
yourself and to others by following sensible health and
safety rules.

## Disabled employees

If you are disabled you should enjoy the same
employment rights and the same protection under the
Health and Safety at Work Act as anyone else.

Where more than 20 people are employed the employer
has a duty to employ a certain quota of registered disabled
people. Where an employer is below his quota he must
take on suitable registered disabled people when a
vacancy occurs. Your employer can often obtain aids from
the government Employment Service to help you do your
work. These aids can be on free permanent loan, and can
include such things as typewriters which have been
adapted, special chairs, etc.

If you are disabled you might wish to take part in the
Job Introduction Scheme, in which you are given a period
of time to adapt to the job.

The staff at your local Jobcentre will help you and give
you advice, and the disablement resettlement officer will
assist you in finding suitable employment.

## Pregnancy and the Health and Safety at Work Act

If you are pregnant you must take special care at work.

Your employer must not ask you to do anything while you are working which would be a hazard to you or your child. The health hazards and maternity are discussed more fully in Chapter 9.

## The Health and Safety Executive
The Health and Safety Executive are a body which enforces the law on health and safety at work. They have under them the inspectors who have powers to enforce the Act on employers who do not comply.

## If you think that there has been a breach of the Act
If you believe that someone has breached the Health and Safety at Work Act you can report the matter to an inspector. The inspector is usually to be found by telephoning your local council offices and asking to be put through to the Health and Safety Department.

TRADE UNION LAW

There is a great deal of law concerning membership of trade unions and of unions themselves. There are particular Acts controlling trade unions, and these Acts will apply to you as an employee if you are a member of a union. Should you experience any problems in your employment you should contact your union representative.

## Trade Union and Labour Relations Act 1974
Trade unions are independent of your employer, and their main objective is to improve and maintain labour relations and to protect the rights of their members. If you are a member of a union you will be asked to pay a sum of money each week to your union. This money is usually deducted at source by your employer. If you are not a union member you are entitled to tell your employer that you do not wish to have this sum deducted.

If you have a complaint which you think the union may

be able to help with, you should contact your union representative who will usually be your shop steward. If you are not successful in settling the problem at this level you should get in touch with your full-time trade union official who will be able to help. It may also be of help to discuss it with other workers and seek their support.

The way your union works will be set out in the union rule book, and the address of the union office will be found in the book. It is up to you as a paid-up member to make use of the help which your union can give you if you are in any kind of trouble in your employment.

## THE WAGES ACT 1986

The Wages Act covers any sums of money that may or may not be deducted by your employer from your wages. The Act says that your employer cannot deduct any money from your wages unless:

1   The deduction is a statutory deduction, such as income tax or national insurance contributions; or such deductions as pension contributions or any arrangement in your contract.
2   You have agreed to the deduction – in writing – beforehand; this kind of deduction might be something like a savings arrangement or a loan repayment to your employer.

This means that your employer cannot simply take sums of money out of your wages without your prior consent.

The **exception** to this rule is that of workers in retail employment. If you work in retail employment your employer can deduct up to one-tenth of the gross amount of pay due to you on any one day for stock or cash shortages. Retail employment means employment where you are carrying out transactions with members of the public, or fellow workers or other individuals in a personal capacity, such as a shop or garage, etc. However, before your employer can deduct any such sums from your wages, he or she must notify you of the amount in writing and that notification must be given to you on a working day. If your employer does not pay you the correct amount of wages or holiday pay under your contract you can take your complaint to an Industrial Tribunal within three months of the date upon which the payment should have been made.

If you have such a complaint, seek advice so that you can put your case in the best way. The Citizen's Advice Bureau or your local Law Centre will be able to help.

# 5.
# SOME OF YOUR BASIC STATUTORY RIGHTS

Most of the rights that you will have as an employee will
come from the Employment Protection (Consolidation)
Act 1978. The EP(C)A itself is made up of older legislation
dealing with employment, gathered up and formed into
the one Act. This Act is amended by Parliament from
time to time, and additions are made to it in the form of
Statutory Instruments which come from European law via
the European Courts of Justice. As with any Act of
Parliament, the EP(C)A has to be interpreted by the
courts and Tribunals, which may vary and produce
different decisions, which in their turn will influence the
way employment is handled generally.

To be protected by the Act, you must:

1   Be an employee, with a contract of service (see
    Chapter 1).
    **and**
2   Work a certain number of hours for there to be such a
    contract.

In order to qualify for statutory rights under the EP(C)A
you must:

1   Be over 16 years of age, and under retirement age.
    **and**

2   Work for more than 16 hours per week.
    **or**
3   Work for more than eight hours per week, provided
    that you have been employed by your employer for at
    least five years.

You will have certain rights in your employment from the
start of your work, and you will become eligible for others
as the length of your service increases.

## RIGHTS FROM THE COMMENCEMENT OF YOUR EMPLOYMENT

### An itemised pay statement

The law says that you are entitled to know what pay you
are receiving, and what deductions are being made from
it, and for what purpose. Deductions will be made by your
employer for tax and national insurance contributions, but
there may also be other sums taken from the final total
which you must have agreed to and must know about.
These extra deductions might be for a private pension
scheme contribution, a personal savings arrangement
between you and your employer, or the repayments on a
personal loan for example. Your employer can only deduct
money from your wages with your written agreement in
advance, or for the purpose of tax and national insurance.
The exception to the above is work in retail employment,
where deductions are made for cash or stock shortages,
but these deductions cannot amount to more than 10 per
cent of your total wages for any one day (see Chapter 4,
page 46).

An itemised pay statement does not have to be a special
form or document; it can be a simple piece of paper, or
even the back of an envelope, as long as it clearly states
the amount that has been taken out of your pay, and for
what reason.

If you are not given a payslip you should ask your
employer to give you one, and if he refuses you can take
your complaint to an Industrial Tribunal within three

months of his refusal, using form **1T1** from Jobcentres or unemployment benefit offices. You should seek advice from the Jobcentre, Citizens Advice Bureau or careers office.

## Time off for antenatal care

If you become pregnant you will be entitled to paid time off to see your doctor or attend medical appointments.

You should notify your employer that you are pregnant, and that you expect to be taking this time off. If your employer asks you, you should show the appointment card or doctor's letter to them so that they can see that it is a genuine appointment (see Chapter 10).

If your employer either refuses to let you have time off for antenatal care, or does not pay you while you are taking that time, you will be able to take them to an Industrial Tribunal and claim that money due to you (see Chapter 11). Again, this claim must be made within three months of the refusal, using form **1T1** from Jobcentres or unemployment benefit offices. You can get advice on your claim from the Jobcentre, Citizens Advice Bureau or careers office.

## Time off for public duties

Your employer must give you time off for public duties, but he does not have to pay you for that time. In practice some employers do not deduct the amount of pay for the time taken, but they have no obligation to pay. Public duties include such things as working as a:

1   Justice of the Peace.
2   Member of a local authority, etc.

Although you will be allowed time off for the above public duties, it must be a reasonable amount of time; this will depend on the circumstances of your employer's business and the effect your absence will have on it.

If you are refused time off to attend to public duties you should complain to an Industrial Tribunal within three

months of the refusal. You can get the form **1T1** from
Jobcentres or Citizens Advice Bureaux.

## Time off for job-hunting or to arrange training when redundant

If you have been given notice that you are to be made
redundant you will be able to take a reasonable amount of
time off from your employment to look for other work, or
to arrange for training. However, you must have received
proper notice of redundancy; you must have been given
the actual date on which your contract will be ended, not
just have been told by your employer that you will be
made redundant at some time in the future (see Chapter
8).

There is no exact amount of time given as reasonable
for you to be expected to take off to look for work, but
should your employer refuse to let you have any time off
you can take the matter to the Industrial Tribunal. The
amount that you can claim in compensation for his refusal
is limited to two-fifths of your week's pay, so this might
point to two days as being a reasonable amount. In any
case, it must be a matter of arrangement with your
employer, so that you can fit in with the running of the
business as far as possible.

If you need to make a claim to the Industrial Tribunal,
it must be made within three months of your employer's
refusal. The form **1T1** may be obtained from a Jobcentre
or unemployment benefit office, and you can get advice on
your claim from Law Centres and Citizens Advice
Bureaux.

## Time off for union duties

Where there is a recognised union in your employment,
you should be allowed reasonable time off to attend union
activities. A reasonable activity could be when you are
acting as a shop steward, or taking part in negotiations on
behalf of the union. However, this provision for time off
for union activities is to be restricted by the new
Employment Bill in due course.

If your employer prevents you from performing your union duties by not allowing you reasonable time off, you may make a claim to the Industrial Tribunal against him on the ground that he has taken 'action short of dismissal' against you and you want compensation. This claim must be made within three months of the action complained of, on form **1T1** which you can get from a Jobcentre or from your union. You will be able to get advice from your union official, and they will support you in your claim.

## Sex discrimination

You have the right not to be discriminated against on the grounds of your sex. This applies to both men and women, and can be applied even before you start work. For instance, you can claim that you have been discriminated against if you answer an advertisement and are told that the future employer will only employ men in his firm and he will not consider you because you are a woman (see Chapter 4, page 37).

If you are discriminated against you can claim against your employer to the Industrial Tribunal on form **1T1** from a Jobcentre or unemployment benefit office. Advice will be given by the Citizens Advice Bureaux, Law Centres or the Equal Opportunities Commission.

## Racial discrimination

An employer must not discriminate against you because of your race, colour or ethnic origin. If you think that your employer is treating you differently to other workers because of your race, or if a future employer refuses to employ you for that reason, again you can take your complaint to the Industrial Tribunal, using form **1T1** from Jobcentres or unemployment benefit offices. You should seek advice from Law Centres, Citizens Advice Bureaux or the Commission for Racial Equality (see Chapter 4, page 39).

## Equal pay

You have the right to be paid the same amount as another

employee doing the same job, similar work or work of
equal value. The law puts a term into an employee's
contract of employment that says that they are not to be
treated 'less favourably' that another employee in the
same employment or doing work which is of equal value.
Although the wording of the Act concerned refers to pay,
the courts have taken pay to include such things as fringe
benefits, status and extra holidays (see Chapter 4, pages
33–35).

If you think that you are being treated unequally in
your employment with regard to pay and conditions of
your contract you can take your complaint to the
Industrial Tribunal, using form **1T1** from Jobcentres and
unemployment benefit offices. As claims of this kind are
extremely complex and the procedure involved is long and
technical, you should get advice as soon as possible from
your local Law Centre, Citizens Advice Bureau or from
the Equal Opportunities Commission (see useful
addresses, page 141, at the end of this book).

## WHEN YOU HAVE BEEN WORKING FOR ONE MONTH

After you have been in your new work for one month you
will be entitled to **one full week's statutory notice**.

If you have any other arrangement in your contract
with your employer which is for a longer period of notice,
you would be entitled to that. For example, if you have
been told that you will have a month's notice at the
termination of your employment, then, if you are
dismissed for anything less than gross misconduct (see
Disciplinary procedure, below), you should be given that
month's notice or paid money in lieu.

If your employer does not stick to his side of the
contract you will have to take action against him in the
county court. However, before you consider taking action
of any kind, you should ask your employer for the money
that you think you are owed; write a letter asking for the
money, and keep a copy in case you have to show it to the

court at a later date. If your employer does not reply, then you might start proceedings against him.

In order to make a claim to the county court you fill in a county court form (see specimen form, page 161) and the court registry will advise you on what to do. If you need further advice you should contact your local Law Centre or Citizens Advice Bureau.

## AFTER 13 WEEKS IN YOUR JOB

When you have been working for 13 weeks you will be entitled to a **written statement of your terms and conditions of employment**. This document is often regarded as the contract, but in fact it is only a written summary of what the contract contains.

Written terms and conditions vary from a simple one-sheet printed form (obtainable at most stationers) to a long and involved series of rules accompanied by an official company handbook. Obviously, the smaller the employer's business the less formal the document will be, but they are all summaries in greater or lesser detail of the employee's contract of employment.

Your terms and conditions should contain such things as:

1 Your name and the date you started work.
2 Your wages/salary, and how you are paid (monthly, 4 weekly).
3 The hours worked, including mention of shifts, etc.
4 Arrangements about sick pay – company sick pay, if any, and an explanation of the statutory sick pay provisions, how you are expected to notify your employer that you will be absent through sickness, and how soon, for example telephone the office before 9.30 am that you will not be working that day.
5 Any pension scheme.
6 Rules about health and safety in your employment and place of work.
7 Rules about uniform or dress requirements.

These are only some of the provisions that might be
included, and it is for your employer to decide what he
considers necessary.

Details of the **grievance procedure** should be
included in the terms and conditions; it should be clearly
stated what you can do if you are unhappy or have a
particular grievance in your work. You should be made
aware of who you can appeal to if your first line of
complaint is not settled, and how to go about appealing
after that. For example:

> If you have a grievance you should complain in the first
> instance to:
> Mrs White, your immediate supervisor,
> and then, if you are not satisfied, to:
> Mr Green, the manager.
> After that, if the matter is still not settled, to:
> Mrs Jones, the personnel director who, together with
> the managing director, will deal with it personally.

The **disciplinary procedure** should be in your written
statement of terms and conditions. You should
understand what will happen if you do not perform your
contract properly, if you disobey your employer's
instructions in any way, or if you break the company
rules. A system of warnings and punishments, in the
shape of suspension from duty with or without pay, or
demotion from your position, should be clearly laid down
and followed by your employer. There should be a list of
things that your employer will treat as gross misconduct
and therefore worthy of your being instantly dismissed,
such as theft, fighting on the premises, breaking the
health and safety rules, disobeying a lawful order given to
you by a superior, etc. Included in the disciplinary rules
should be the line of possible appeal in the event of your
being dismissed, how you can appeal against being
dismissed and the time-limit for any such appeal. For
example:

If you wish to appeal against your dismissal, you should do so in writing, to the chairman, Mr A. Hill, within seven days of receipt of your dismissal letter. An appeal hearing will be arranged and you will be notified of the date. You may, if you wish, be accompanied by a member of staff, a relation or a union official of your own choosing.

You may be asked to sign a copy of your terms and conditions when they are given to you. This does not establish them as being a contract – it simply indicates that you have read them.

Not all employers will issue you with terms and conditions of your employment. This may not be intentional; they may simply be unaware that you should have them. If they are a small employer they may not want to have to deal with the paperwork involved. Although you should have terms and conditions, as long as your employment is progressing well they will not be needed. You do have the right to complain to an Industrial Tribunal that you have not been given terms and conditions, but the chances are that your employer would not be pleased at your doing so, and you might lose your job as a result. A Tribunal can establish for you what the terms and conditions should have been by looking at what is custom and practice in your contract at the time, and deciding accordingly.

## AFTER WORKING FOR 26 WEEKS

When you have been working for 26 weeks (six months) you will have the right to written reasons for your dismissal if your contract is terminated by your employer. (It is intended that this will be brought up to two years by the Employment Bill.) This means that your employer must put in writing why and for what reason he decided to dismiss you. You may not like the reasons, but you are entitled to get them. As you cannot claim unfair dismissal, etc., until you have worked for two years for your employer (see Chapter 4), the reason will only be useful to you for your own satisfaction or for any dispute you may have with your employer over money in lieu of notice. The reason your employer gives for your dismissal may also be helpful when your unemployment benefit is being considered by the DSS.

If your employer unreasonably refuses to give you written reasons for your dismissal you can complain to an Industrial Tribunal, and you will be compensated by the amount of two weeks' gross pay. But you can only complain to the Tribunal if your employer has 'unreasonably' refused to give them to you. He is supposed to give them to you within 14 days of your request (either verbal or in writing), but often an employer will promise to do it and then forget, or put the matter out of his mind; if he does so and it drags on, it will be for you to argue that that delay in itself constitutes an unreasonable refusal.

If you wish to make a complaint to an Industrial Tribunal, you can do so on form **1T1** from the Jobcentre or the local unemployment benefit office. You may get advice on your claim from Law Centres or Citizens Advice Bureaux.

## Some basic statutory rights you will have when you work

*When you start work* ▶ Itemised pay statements.
Right to time off for antenatal care.
Time off for public duties.

*After one month\** ▶ Right to statutory notice.

*After 13 weeks\** ▶ Right to a written statement of the terms and conditions of the contract.

*After 26 weeks\** ▶ Right to written reasons if you (at present) are dismissed.

▼

When you have worked for *two years\** continuously in the same employment you have extra rights under the law (see Chapter 6).

\*These times can be changed by the government (the Secretary of State for Employment).

# 6.
# YOUR RIGHTS AFTER TWO YEARS IN THE SAME EMPLOYMENT

When you have worked in the same employment continuously for two years you will be eligible for further rights under the Employment Protection (Consolidation) Act 1978. Until you have worked for your employer for two years you cannot make a claim to an Industrial Tribunal that you have been unfairly dismissed, you cannot claim that you have been forced to resign from your job because of your employer's conduct and you will not be eligible for a redundancy payment if you are made redundant. All these rights depend upon the length of service that you have had – **two full years**.

## DO YOU QUALIFY?

You will be eligible for the above rights in your employment if you are an employee, i.e. if you are employed under a contract of service by your employer. Most employees who work have the right to make a claim to an Industrial Tribunal under the Act, but the qualification depends on the following:

1   You must be an employee.
2   In the majority of cases you will need to have had two years' continuous service.

3   You must work:
      over 16 hours per week for your employer and have
      worked for two continuous years.
      **or**
      Over 8 hours per week for your employer and have
      worked for over five continuous years.
4   You must be over 16 years of age and under
      retirement age.

If you fulfill the above qualifications you will be able to
bring a claim to an Industrial Tribunal (see Chapter 11).
   If you intend to bring a claim to a Tribunal you will, in
most cases, have **three months** from the date of the
termination of your contract or the date on which the act
of which you are complaining takes place. So if you think
that you may have a case, get advice as soon as possible –
you must not get out of time, or the Tribunal will not be
able to hear your claim.

---

**Do you qualify for rights under the EP(C)A 1978?**

| | | |
|---|---|---|
| *Length of time you have worked* | ▶ | You have worked for two years continuously in the same employment. |
| *Hours* | ▶ | Over 16 hours per week or between 8–16 hours per week if you have been working for over five full years. |
| *Age* | ▶ | You are over 16 years and under retirement age. Soon to be 65 for both men and women. |
| *The kind of jobs in which you do not qualify* | ▶ | The police, the armed forces, crown servants, share fishermen etc. |

## Workers who do not qualify

You will not qualify for rights under the EP(C)A if:

1 You are not an employee; for instance, if you are a subcontractor, a freelance agent or someone who is in business on their own.
2 If you have not worked for your employer for two continuous years.
3 If you normally work less than 16 hours per week and have not worked for five continuous years.
4 If you work for less than 8 hours per week.
5 If you have reached retiring age before your contract is terminated (you may complain that you have been unfairly dismissed at any age if your dismissal is on account of trade union activities).
6 If your contract was for a fixed term and it has been agreed in writing that you will not claim for unfair dismissal, although you will then be able to claim for other rights in these circumstances.
7 You are a member of the police force or the armed services.
8 You are the master or crew of a fishing vessel and are paid solely by a share of the profits.
9 You do all your work outside the United Kingdom (except for people who work on the continental shelf, such as oil workers, etc.).
10 You are a crown servant or a member of the staff of the House of Lords.

## THE RIGHT NOT TO BE UNFAIRLY DISMISSED

**Dismissal** means that your contract of employment is terminated by your employer. If there is no dismissal there can be no claim for unfair dismissal. If you give in your notice you are not dismissed – you are ending the contract by your own choice.

## What constitutes dismissal?

1   If you leave your employment there is no dismissal; you are terminating the contract of employment.
2   If you and your employer come to an agreement that the contract is to end and between you decide the date and the terms of the parting, again there is no dismissal.
3   If something happens outside the contract which is not the fault of you or your employer; for instance, if you were to have a serious accident that prevented you from doing your work, then the contract would come to an end. This is called frustration of the contract, and is not a dismissal.
4   Your employer has given you notice and, while you are working out that notice, you find another job. If you agree with your employer that you will leave the job before the end of the notice period, then the original dismissal disappears.

Sometimes it is not made completely clear by an employer that they intend to terminate the contract of the employee. For instance:

Mrs Browne, who was the owner of a boutique, came in on Saturday morning at 9.35 am and found that her employee Janet was waiting on the pavement as the manager Miss Green had not yet arrived to open up the shop. Mrs Browne was very cross at what she saw as misconduct by Miss Green, and said to her 'I shall have to dismiss you.' Miss Green took this to mean that she was dismissed, and claimed unfair dismissal on the strength of it. The Tribunal considered that the words used by Mrs Browne did not mean 'I am dismissing you now' but 'If you do this again I will dismiss you in the future.' Miss Green's claim did not succeed; the Tribunal said there was no dismissal as Miss Green had resigned.

In order for there to be a dismissal there has to be a definite action on the part of the employer to terminate the contract and that action has to be accepted as such by the employee.

## THE RIGHT TO A REDUNDANCY PAYMENT

If you have worked continuously in the same employment for over two years and you are over the age of 18 you will be entitled to a payment if you are made redundant by your employer.

To qualify for a redundancy payment you must have been dismissed by reason of redundancy by your employer. They must terminate your contract in exactly the same way as in any other dismissal (except dismissal for gross misconduct, i.e. summary or instant dismissal); you will be entitled to notice as in any other dismissal, and if you are not given notice you should receive money in lieu in the usual way.

Redundancy is a right which depends upon the length of your service with your employer, and is calculated in various stages as your length of service increases in years (see Chapter 8). However, if you resign from your employment you will not be entitled to claim a redundancy payment from your employer.

Make sure that you clearly understand what the arrangements are if your employer says he is making you redundant. Do not leave before the date he gives as your termination date without making sure that you will not endanger your right to your redundancy payment.

## YOUR RIGHTS DURING LAY-OFF OR SHORT-TIME WORKING

At a time when work is short and your employer cannot keep all the workforce employed, they may choose to lay people off or put them on short-time working until things get better and can go back to normal.

If you are laid-off there will be no work for you to do,

and you will not receive any wages from your employer until the period of lay-off ends. If you are put on short-time working you will have your hours of work reduced temporarily so that you will be receiving less than half a week's pay.

When you have been laid-off for over four weeks you will have the right to claim a redundancy payment from your employer. The procedure for claiming redundancy is a complex procedure and is explained fully in Chapter 8.

## GUARANTEE PAYMENTS

If you are not given work by your employer for a whole day which you would normally work, you may be entitled to a 'guarantee payment' from your employer. This is a minimum 'fall back' payment made to employees who have more than **three months**' service with the same employer.

The amount of guarantee payment is calculated by:

1 $\dfrac{\text{A normal week's pay}}{\text{Average normal working hours per week}}$ = Hourly rate of pay

2 Hourly rate × Number of hours in workless day = Amount of guarantee payment per day

There is a maximum figure for the guarantee payment which is set by law and is increased from 1 April each year.

1 You will be entitled to five days' payments in a period of three months.
2 If you normally work less than five days per week you can only claim for the days you would have been working in the three-month period.
3 If your hours vary from week to week, then an average is taken for the last three months.

If you are eligible for a guarantee payment you should make enquiries at your local unemployment benefit office.

## MATERNITY RIGHTS

When you become pregnant, if you have been continuously employed in the same employment for two years when you arrive at the **11th week before the expected date of confinement**, you will have certain rights under the maternity provisions of the Act, such as:

1 The right to paid time off for antenatal care.
2 The right not to be unfairly dismissed on the grounds of your pregnancy.
3 The right to return to your job after maternity leave.
4 The right to be paid statutory maternity pay (SMP) if you qualify.
5 The right not to be discriminated against because of your sex when you are pregnant.
6 The right to return to work after having a baby.

You will be entitled to 29 weeks leave beginning with the actual week of confinement.

The rules governing maternity are set out in detail in Chapter 10.

## YOUR RIGHTS WHEN THERE IS A TAKEOVER OR SALE OF THE BUSINESS

When an employer sells the business, the contracts of employment of the people working for it are protected by the Transfer of Undertakings Regulations. These Regulations came from European law, and are intended to protect you if you are dismissed because of the sale or transfer of the business for which you work.

If the business, or part of it, is transferred from one owner to another there cannot be any arrangement between the two employers that limits your rights under the Regulations. So, if your employer sells the shop in which you are working and the new owner arranges with the current owner that you will be dismissed because you will not be needed, then, if you have sufficient service, you will be entitled to some sort of compensation, either in the form of a redundancy payment or compensation for unfair dismissal, for your dismissal.

The Regulations say that you must not be dismissed because of the transfer or sale of a business. The same thing will apply if the terms of your contract (such as hours, pay, etc.) are drastically varied when the business is sold. The Regulations provide that:

1   Employees of the seller of a business will have their contracts of employment automatically transferred to the buyer of the business on the same terms and conditions.
2   The continuity of service of these employees will be preserved. This means that if you have worked for your old employer for four years when they sell the business, and at a later date you are made redundant, those four years with the original employer will count when you calculate the amount of redundancy payment you will receive (see Chapter 8).

The Regulations only apply when a commercial undertaking is transferred from one owner to another. This may be the whole of the business or part of it; for example, a transfer under the Regulations might be:

1   Where all of a trader's business (such as four launderettes, or two branches of a garage business) or a partnership is sold or transferred to another person or company.
2   Where a company, or part of it, is taken over by someone else (perhaps a particular branch of a chain of shops might be bought by a national company and become part of a national group). When this occurs there must be a sale of the assets of the business, not just a transfer of the shares.

3    Where two separate companies are merged together
     and form a completely new company, such as in the
     case of Brown & Co. and John Voctor Ltd, who were
     bought by a third individual and became Smithson &
     Co. Ltd.

The Regulations apply equally to any business, from the
multinational to the small one-person concern, so you
might have 1,000 employees being transferred, or one –
the rules will apply to them all.

## Exceptions
The Regulations do **not** apply to:

1    Share-transfers – a company's shares can be
     transferred without the business being affected.
2    When only the assets are sold, for example when only
     the machinery is sold and not the business as a going
     concern.
3    Transfers of a business outside the United Kingdom,
     or to people who normally work outside the United
     Kingdom.

## Transfers made when the business is in financial difficulties
When an employer is in financial difficulties and a
receiver or administrator has been appointed, the
company might not be transferred as a whole; only part of
it might be set up on its own, to see if it can be made to
pay. This is called hiving down.
   Part of the company will be transferred to a subsidiary
company and, if it can be set on its feet, it will then be
sold as a going concern. If you are working for the part of
the business that is treated in this way, then your rights
under the Regulations will be the same as if the whole
company had been transferred.

## Your position when there is a transfer of a business
Your contract of employment should not be materially

affected by the fact that your employer has sold the
business over your head. The only thing that might be
affected by the transfer would be any occupational
pension that you might have had with your old employer;
this is not necessarily transferred when a business is sold,
and you might have to make other arrangements for your
pension.

If your contract of employment is radically changed by
your new employer, you may have cause for complaint.
For example, if:

1   The new employer **changes your hours** – they tell
    you that in future you will work different shifts, or on
    different days to those you have always worked before.
    This may be viewed as a fundamental change in the
    terms of your employment.
2   There is a **reduction in your pay**, for whatever
    reason, or there is a restructuring of the grading
    system which results in your losing a possible wage
    rise.
3   There is a reorganisation of jobs and you find that you
    are being **demoted from your position** to a job
    with less responsibility or status.

Then you could make a claim to an Industrial Tribunal,
on the basis that this fundamental change in your
contract is unacceptable to you and that by changing the
contractual arrangements your new employer has
breached the contract or broken his side of the bargain.
However, it is no good complaining of small alterations in
your contract; for example, your new employer may like
to change the seating arrangements in the offices, or ask
that you wear a uniform in future, and so on.

If you are really unhappy about such changes, use any
grievance procedure that may be set out in your written
terms and conditions; or if you do not have anything in
writing, talk it over with your new employer and see if you
can negotiate with them. They may be unaware that you
do not like the changes. Always try to negotiate when

there is any problem, as it can avoid further trouble and
may lead to better industrial relations. If there is a union
in your firm you should talk it over with your
representative and let them negotiate for you. If there is
no union, there may be a workers' representative who may
be able to help.

## If the change in your contract is serious and fundamental

If you consider that the change that your new employer is
proposing is really serious and will affect your working
conditions, pay, etc., to such an extent that you cannot
accept it, then you may be able to claim to an Industrial
Tribunal that you have been constructively dismissed (see
Chapter 7).

If you decide that this is the position, you will have to
decide quickly what you are going to do:

1  Resign your job and claim that you have been
   constructively dismissed.
   **or**
2  Accept the changes that your employer has proposed
   and go on in your job under what will be a varied
   contract.

You should weigh up the position carefully, because if you
do not accept the changes in your contract your only
recourse (if negotiation has failed) is to resign and make
your claim to an Industrial Tribunal. This will mean that
you will be without a job and your unemployment benefit
may also be suspended.

The arguments which arise when someone is dismissed
on the transfer of an undertaking are very complicated. If
your employer can establish that they dismissed you
because of an 'economic, technical or organisational
reason entailing changes in the workforce', your dismissal
may be proved fair. In these circumstances you might be
entitled to a redundancy payment, but it would be a
matter to be argued at the Tribunal. A lot will depend on

the time at which you were dismissed, and if the Tribunal considers that your employer acted reasonably in dismissing you. What is also important, of course, is which of the two employers actually dismissed you, the old or the new. If there is any uncertainty, you should put in a claim against them both and let the Tribunal decide which one will be responsible for any payment in compensation or redundancy.

This is an extremely complicated area of law and it is constantly changing. Get advice – your local Jobcentre or Citizens Advice Bureau may be able to help in the first instance, or an employment law specialist solicitor or Law Centre. If you intend to make a claim you will have three months from the date of the termination of your employment in which to send in your application to the Tribunal.

# 7.
# DISMISSAL – FAIR OR UNFAIR?

If you qualify under the Employment Protection (Consolidation) Act 1978 by reason of your length of service, hours, age, occupation, etc., you will be able to make a claim for unfair dismissal to an Industrial Tribunal, and, if you succeed, you may get compensation.

## WHEN WERE YOU DISMISSED?

In order for you to be able to make a claim, there must have been a dismissal. When you have been dismissed it is vital to find out the effective date of termination – that is, the date when your contract of employment came to an end. It is necessary to do this for the following reasons:

1   You need to establish how long you have been working for your employer, i.e. how many years' service you can count towards
    • qualifying under the Act, and
    • calculating any compensation you may get.
2   Putting your claim into the Industrial Tribunal to claim for unfair dismissal, etc. You will have **three months** from the date of the termination of your contract in which to register any claim.
3   It is important to establish the date of termination as you may be excluded from making a claim because of your age. If you have reached retiring age before the date on which your contract ends, you will not be able to claim.
4   You will be able to ask your employer for written reasons for your dismissal after the date of the

termination. You will have to have worked for the
same employer for 26 weeks to be eligible for this right.
(The 26 weeks will become two years when the
Employment Bill becomes law.)

See Chapter 3.

## DISMISSALS THAT ARE FAIR

The dismissal of an employee can be fair if the employer
can show that they acted reasonably in the circumstances
and followed proper procedure in the actual dismissal. If
your employer does not act reasonably and if they do not
follow proper procedure, then the dismissal will be viewed
as unfair.

The following kinds of, or reasons for, dismissal might
be fair, and an employer would be entitled to dismiss you.

### Capability and qualification
Dismissal because of your lack of **capability or
qualifications** to do the work that you are employed to
do.

*Capability*    Usually capability falls into two kinds:

1    An employee is unable to do their job because of ill
     health.
2    The employee is simply incompetent or being lazy or
     not pulling their weight.

It is sometimes difficult to distinguish between these two
kinds of capability. Obviously if you have been working for
a long time it will be difficult to say that you are
incompetent; but if you come into a job as a new worker, it
may be that you do not, or cannot, measure up to what is
required of you in the work.

James Davidson was a machinist on the factory floor.
He had worked for his employer for five years, was a

good worker, never clocking in late and seldom having any time off for sickness, etc. In August he was promoted to foreman and was in charge of six other men in his department. At first he was able to cope with the work, but gradually problems began to develop and Mr Davidson became very stressed by the responsibility. He started getting to the factory late in the morning because he was sleeping badly, and was away sick on several occasions with depression and stress-related illness. His employer decided that he was not efficient as a worker in general, and a foreman in particular, and dismissed him at the end of October.

Mr Davidson went to a Tribunal and it was found that he had been unfairly dismissed because his employer had not looked into the matter, had not made proper enquiries as to why the work wasn't going well, and had not given Mr Davidson time to get himself together and improve. Mr Davidson said that he found that he could not cope with the increased responsibility of being foreman and would like his job back on the factory floor. The employer agreed to the suggestion and Mr Davidson got his original job back.

In this case the employee was not being lazy or wilfully absent; he was simply not capable of doing the more responsible job that was given to him. But, as the Tribunal said, his employer should have found out the real reason before sacking him.

The case of Dianne Jones, on the other hand, was quite different. Miss Jones had worked as a machinist in a clothing factory after leaving school three years previously and was generally considered a good worker. During the Christmas break after her third year at work she met a young man who had been in trouble with the police and had recently been dismissed from his job. The relationship progressed, and in February of that year Dianne moved into a small flat with him.

Gradually it was noticed by her workmates and her supervisor that Dianne was becoming more careless in her work. She made mistakes which caused disruption and, on one occasion, damage to a machine. She was inclined to arrive at work late and came back late after the lunch-break. Her work fell behind the other workers and she frequently held up the overall work process, which made her unpopular. In April the manager called her into the office and officially warned her that if she didn't pull her socks up she would face disciplinary action. She continued behaving in the same way. Eventually, after more warnings and a period of suspension, she was dismissed in September.

She complained to an Industrial Tribunal that her dismissal was unfair, but it was found to be fair as Dianne was perfectly capable of doing her job but was behaving badly; therefore her employer was perfectly correct in dismissing her for that behaviour.

*Qualification*    Qualifications may be required of you in order that you can do the job. For instance, you may be required to hold a clean driving licence in order to drive the company car.

Mr Blackman worked for the Post Office, and was asked to take an aptitude test agreed by the union in order to be appointed to a permanent post as a telegraph and postal worker. He took the test and failed. The Post Office allowed him to take the test three times but he failed every time, so they dismissed him. It was decided that this was a fair dismissal as he did not have (and could not get) the required qualifications for the job.

## Dismissal because of your conduct

Reasons for dismissal which are for conduct include a very wide variety of acts. If they are clearly acts of misconduct an employer will be justified in dismissing an employee, and the dismissal will be fair. Misconduct can include such things as:

1  Disobeying the employer's rules.
2  Bad time-keeping.
3  Absenteeism.
4  Disobeying an order given by the employer.
5  Fighting, theft, drunkenness.
6  Refusing to do a particular job.
7  Incompetence or laziness.

However, you do not have to obey an order from your employer if that order is not lawful or is contrary to public policy.

## Dismissal because you are redundant
A dismissal by reason of redundancy is a fair reason. If employees are made redundant then those dismissals will always be fair (see Chapter 8).

## Dismissal because you are prevented in law from doing your work
The majority of dismissals under this heading involve employees who are doing the job of a driver of some kind (van driver, lorry driver, chauffeur) and who are banned from driving or lose their licence. This situation makes it impossible for the employer to go on employing them lawfully, and the dismissal in those circumstances must be fair.

## Dismissal for some other substantial reason
Whatever the reason your employer chooses as a reason for dismissing you, it must be a **substantial** reason; in other words, it must be a serious and proper reason which they must honestly believe to be important enough to warrant dismissing you. For instance:

An employer dismisses a man for not agreeing to a reasonable change in the terms and conditions of the contract. The change was simply an adjustment of the factory's starting-time to fit in with a change in the local bus timetable to assist workers getting to work.

The employer had given six weeks' notice of the change and only one employee refused to agree.

A kitchen assistant employed in a large establishment was totally set in his ways. He had worked there for 12 years. A new deputy head chef was appointed, and at his instigation new machinery was installed in the kitchen. Naturally, this meant that certain things had to be changed and the remaining processes, like vegetable preparation and chip-frying, had to be reorganised to fit in. The new chef found that the kitchen assistant would not do as he was asked, and the kitchen assistant instantly disliked the chef and thought him an 'upstart'. The result was constant warfare which upset the smooth running of the kitchen. They were both warned by their employer.

Eventually, the manager had to be called when there was an incident when each was threatening the other with violence. After much discussion it was decided that this could not go on, and the kitchen assistant was sacked, on the basis that he had been given the opportunity to fit in but had not done so.

An employee was dismissed because they suffered from epileptic fits. During these fits the employee unknowingly became very violent towards other people in the vicinity. The employer took the view that this could be a danger to any other employee who happened to be near when a fit was taking place.

When a farm was taken over the new farmer-employer wanted to employ his own son on the farm, so he dismissed the original farm worker.

Under the heading 'any other substantial reason' the reason for your dismissal must really be justified by your employer; it must be a serious and/or unavoidable reason which they sincerely believe in at the time that you are dismissed.

Although the above reasons for dismissal are potentially fair reasons, your employer must behave reasonably when they actually dismiss you. Notice should be given, and any appropriate procedures (such as consultation or disciplinary procedures) should be followed. If the way you are dismissed is not reasonable your dismissal may be unfair.

## DISMISSALS WHICH MIGHT BE UNFAIR

### Conduct
Conduct dismissals are of two kinds:

1   Misconduct of a lesser degree.
2   Gross misconduct.

*Misconduct*   Behaviour that comes under the heading of misconduct can be any number of things – getting in late, talking when you should be at work, being rude to customers, leaving your workplace untidy, not following instructions given to you by someone in authority, being careless in your work, forgetting to do tasks that have been asked of you, and so on. The list can be endless and can vary from employer to employer, but in every case an employer who intends to dismiss an employee for misconduct must follow reasonable procedure.

1   You must be made aware by your employer that what you are doing is not in accordance with his wishes.
2   You must be given warnings about your conduct so that you can improve. A warning should not be a punishment; it should tell you what you are doing wrong so that you may take the opportunity of putting it right in future. It should also clearly tell you that if you do not make an effort to improve in future you will be in danger of losing your job. Warnings for misconduct can be both verbal and written, and it is up to your employer to warn you in a reasonable manner.

3    Before you are dismissed your employer should
     consider everything very carefully. They should
     discuss the conduct carefully with everyone
     concerned, and above all you should be given the
     opportunity to put your side of the case. After they
     have gone through all these steps and there is no other
     way out, then there should be a dismissal.

Mrs Johnson, a hairdresser working in a small salon in
a market town, started to get in to work late more and
more frequently. Her employer depended on her being
there to take her customers at 8.30 am, but she was
frequently late. She was given three or four verbal
warnings about her lateness, without any effect.
Finally, her employer gave her a written warning to the
effect that if she was late again she would be sacked.
She improved for a week or two, but after a bank
holiday weekend she was late again. Her employer
asked for an explanation but she could not give one, so
she was dismissed.

There is no set of rules or laws governing warnings, but the
Advisory, Conciliation and Arbitration Service (ACAS)
have produced a code of practice on industrial relations
which covers warnings and other disciplinary procedures.
The code of practice is available as a guideline for
employers, and Tribunals consider what it has to say
when they are making their decisions. Copies of the ACAS
code may be obtained through Jobcentres.

*Gross misconduct*    Gross misconduct is conduct by an
employee that merits immediate dismissal without notice
– fighting, theft, disobeying a lawful order given to you by
your employer or someone in authority, etc. If you are
dismissed in this way for reasons of gross misconduct and
you believe that your dismissal is unfair you can ask an
Industrial Tribunal to give a decision on the matter.
    If you are dismissed for gross misconduct you will not
be entitled to any payment such as notice money or

holiday pay. Should the Tribunal find that your dismissal was unfair you will be able to claim compensation and the amount of these payments from your employer.

Mrs Shift was dismissed from her employment as a factory operative because she was seen hitting another employee in the face, after which a fight developed which lasted until a foreman managed to separate them. As Mrs Shift was a long-serving employee the manager said that she should have set an example, so she was dismissed immediately without notice. The other person was given a final written warning, but continued working at the factory.

Mrs Shift complained to the Tribunal that her dismissal was unfair because the other employee had started the fight by calling her names and following her around the factory shouting at her in front of other employees. She said that finally she was so provoked that she struck out blindly, not meaning to start a fight, but that the other employee had retaliated by blacking her eye and scratching her on the arm. The Tribunal heard that the management had not enquired properly into the reason for the fight, or the circumstances in which it started; neither had they given Mrs Shift a proper opportunity to state her side of the affair; and finally, they had not taken into consideration in the proper manner her long service and previously good character. They found that she had been unfairly dismissed, she was awarded compensation and the sum of money to which she would have been entitled in lieu of her notice was paid to her.

In any dismissal – and particularly in the case of gross misconduct dismissals (which are usually summary or instant dismissals) – your employer should make proper investigations into what happened. You should clearly understand what you may or may not have done, and above all you should be allowed to give the management your side of the story. If your employer does not do all these things your dismissal will almost certainly be unfair.

*Capability – sickness*   An employer should not dismiss
you simply because you are off sick. You can be dismissed
if your sickness genuinely makes you incapable of doing
your job, but your employer must make full enquiries into
the situation before you are dismissed.

While you are absent from your job through sickness
you should keep in contact with your employer –
you should notify them of the progress of your illness, any
hospital appointments you may be attending and, above
all, when you or your doctor think that you will be likely to
return. There are no hard and fast rules about how long
someone can be off sick without it affecting their
employment; so much depends on circumstances, such as:

1   How often have you been sick before?
2   How serious is your illness?
3   Will you be permanently affected by your illness?
4   How large or small is the employer's business?
5   How long could they reasonably be expected to keep
    your job open?

All these things vary from case to case.

The state of the employee's illness should be known to
the employer, and the possibility of their recovery looked
at in detail. Only after careful study of all these factors
should the employer consider dismissal of an employee
who is absent through sickness.

Mrs Pound worked in a shop, selling dress material.
During the Christmas rush she moved a display stand
containing seven large rolls of material, and in the
course of this operation strained her back. She reported
this accident to her superior and was sent home. It was
found that the injury to her back was more serious than
was at first thought and she had to have a series of
treatments at the hospital, followed by visits to the
physiotherapy department for some weeks. Mrs Pound

kept in touch with her employers by sending in her certificates and by regularly telephoning people at work to let them know how she was getting on.

After five months her employer again became very busy and decided to sack Mrs Pound and replace her. Mrs Pound was very upset at being dismissed in this way, particularly as the day before her dismissal letter arrived her doctor had told her that she could go back to work in three weeks' time. She telephoned her employer and told the personnel manager this, but she was told that the dismissal had 'gone through' and the decision could not be reversed.

It was found that the dismissal was unfair because the employer had not made proper enquiries as to the date upon which Mrs Pound could have returned in the first place, and had not behaved reasonably when given the relevant information.

## Refusal to give the job back after maternity leave

When you leave to have a baby your contract is not automatically terminated; you remain an employee of your employer – an employee who is absent by reason of taking maternity leave.

The Employment Protection (Consolidation) Act 1978 gives you the right to return to work after you have had a baby. If you have fulfilled all the requirements to qualify for that right and your employer refuses to allow you to return to work, that will be taken to be an unfair dismissal.

The rights given to you by the state when you have a baby will be the minimum; they will be the least that your employer can give you in the circumstances. If there are any other rights that you are entitled to under your contract, those rights will also be due to you.

1   If your employer denies you your extra or contractual maternity rights, you can ask for them in the county court.

2   If your employer denies you any of your statutory
    maternity rights you will be able to complain to an
    Industrial Tribunal.

Your maternity rights, the required qualifications for
those rights and the remedies when they are not allowed
to you are discussed at length in Chapter 10.

## Unfair selection for redundancy

A dismissal by reason of redundancy is in itself a fair
dismissal, but if the wrong person is selected to be made
redundant that can be an unfair dismissal. If you think
that you have been selected for redundancy unfairly you
should look carefully at all the circumstances:

1   Were you employed in the **same business or
    undertaking** as other people who were not chosen
    for redundancy?
2   Were there other people working in the **same sort of
    job** as you who were kept on by your employer?
3   When choosing to make you redundant, did your
    employer follow the **proper procedure**, either
    written down or agreed?

If you can answer these questions and see that your
employer has not behaved reasonably in their selection of
you as an employee to be made redundant, you may take
your complaint to the Industrial Tribunal.

A complaint of unfair selection for redundancy has to
be made to the Industrial Tribunal within three months of
the date of the termination of your employment. If you
think that you have been unfairly selected for redundancy
you should get advice, as such a claim is difficult for the
employee to pursue. Your local law centre or Citizens
Advice Bureau may be able to help. (Redundancy is
discussed in detail in Chapter 8.)

## Dismissal for trade union activities

The EP(C)A gives you the right not to be dismissed for

becoming, or seeking to become, a trade union member or for engaging in trade union activities.

1  If your employer dismisses you because he is of the opinion that you are intending to become a member of a trade union, that dismissal will be unfair. Sometimes an employer will disguise the real reason for a dismissal by calling it by another name; for instance, if they believe that you have made enquiries of a union about joining, or have filled in a membership form for a union, they may say that you are to be made redundant and get rid of you. That way the employers would not have to employ a union member in their business and they would avoid the large amounts of compensation payable to an employee who is dismissed because they wanted to become a union member. If you think your dismissal was for reasons connected with union membership, you can make a claim to the Industrial Tribunal.

2  If your employer dismisses you because you are taking part in union activities such as meetings or ballots or because of your duties as a shop steward, that dismissal will be unfair. However industrial action does not count as union activity. You are, at present (November 1989), entitled to reasonable time off for union activities and your employer must not discipline you if you take it, but this will be limited by the Employment Bill in due course.

3  To be a member of a union you will have to pay a subscription or due. It is usual for an employer to propose that people pay the sum of the union due – so much per week – into a charity instead of their being a union member. You have the right to refuse to pay any of these sums, and your employer must not try to force you to pay them.

4  You have the right not to be dismissed for union membership or activities, and you also have the right not to have **action short of dismissal** taken against you for the same reasons. Action short of

dismissal means things like threats against you, discrimination in promotion, denying you opportunities for training, or transferring you from one job to another. In one case denying an employee a parking permit was found to be action short of dismissal.

If you think that you have a complaint under the heading of trade union membership or activities you can go to the Industrial Tribunal — get advice from the union, who may help you with your claim. Virtually all employees can make such a complaint, regardless of their age, length of service or hours of work.

People who cannot complain are the self-employed, the armed forces, the police, share fishermen and people who work abroad.

## Fixed-term contract
A fixed-term contract can be either:

1   A contract for a particular length of time.
    **or**
2   A contract for a particular purpose.

*Contract for a particular length of time*   If you have a fixed-term contract for a year or more, and if your employer does not renew that contract at the end of the period, you will have been unfairly dismissed.

This unfair dismissal provision is to stop employers taking on people with fixed-term contracts and getting rid of them at the end of each contract, thereby avoiding the protection given to employees by the Act. For instance, an employee could be taken on for a series of one-year contracts such that they never add up the amount of service required for them to be able to claim their rights under the Act. So, if you are employed on a fixed-term contract and you have two years' service, if your contract is not renewed when it ends you will be unfairly dismissed and will be able to claim to the Industrial Tribunal. The claim must be lodged within three months of the date of the termination of your contract.

If you enter into a contract which is a fixed-term contract for more than one year, you can elect to **sign away** your right to claim unfair dismissal at the end of the contract if it is not renewed. This decision on your part has to be in writing and is agreed between you and your employer.

The question of claiming unfair dismissal on the termination of a fixed-term contract is somewhat complicated, so get advice from your local Law Centre, your trade union or Citizens Advice Bureau.

*Contract for a particular purpose*   If you are employed under a contract for a particular purpose or a particular job, the chances are that it will not be a fixed-term contract for the purposes of the Act and you will not have the right to claim unfair dismissal at the end. An example of such a contract is someone who is employed to work on the repair of a ship. When the job is finished and the ship sails, it will be said that the contract has automatically come to an end and there is no termination. Or the case of a temporary teacher employed 'only as long as funds are available'; when the funds run out the contract ends and there is no claim for unfair dismissal.

## Constructive dismissal

Constructive dismissal is when your employer's conduct or behaviour breaches the contract of employment and you cannot continue working for them. There are many ways in which an employer can breach or sever the contract, and each case must be judged from an individual standpoint.

You cannot claim that you have been constructively dismissed by your employer unless their action is a significant breach of the contract. The breach of your contract can be an **actual breach taking place now** or an **anticipatory breach taking place in the future**.

1   Whatever the breach on the part of your employer, it
    must be a **fundamental** breach going to the root of
    your contract. In other words, it is a serious alteration
    of your contract.
2   When your employer has breached, or is going to
    breach, your contract you can try to negotiate with
    them, or resign and claim that you have been
    constructively dismissed.
3   You must make up your mind about whether or not
    you can accept the breach or alteration in your
    contract quickly. If you feel that you cannot accept it
    you must move quickly and resign. If you do not resign
    and you work under the changed contract, you will be
    considered to have accepted the variation and the
    alteration will become part of your contract.

The following are examples of what might be considered
**constructive dismissals**:

Ann was manager of a shop. Her employer told her that
the following week she was to be demoted to till
operative, her pay would be reduced and she would lose
status. She decided that this alteration was
unacceptable.

Tony was working night shifts for a wholesale
newsagents, 9.00 pm to 5.30 am. His employer told him
that his hours were to be changed to 7.30 pm to 4.00
am. There was no change in the wages, but the change
in hours was impossible owing to family commitments.

John worked in a night club. He arrived late one
morning after arranging this the night before with the
manager. The owner, who was on the premises when he
walked in, immediately started to shout and swear at
him for being late. John thought that he had better get
out of the room until the owner calmed down, then
explain later, so he made for the door. The owner
shouted at him that he could 'get out'. John argued at

the Tribunal that that was dismissal, but the employer said it was not. The Tribunal found that even if it was not actual dismissal by the owner, John could consider himself constructively dismissed by his employer's behaviour.

These are only some of the many examples of the different things that can come under constructive dismissal.

If you have any really serious variations of your contract, you should seek advice very quickly – if you do not act quickly your employer can say that you **accepted** that change. For instance:

1   If Ann had started working on the till without argument, she would have accepted the change.
2   If Tony had turned up and worked on the 7.30 pm shift he would be thought to have accepted the changed shifts.
3   When John's employer gave him verbal abuse, if he had gone on working for him it would have been thought that John believed that being abused was a normal part of his contract and had accepted it.

When you are faced with a serious and fundamental breach of your contract you should think carefully of all the implications involved, such as:

1   Can you put up with the change?
2   Can you get other work?
3   Will you get unemployment benefit if you resign?

and so on. You will need to get advice and assistance if you are going to make a claim to the Industrial Tribunal, and your local Citizens Advice Bureau may be able to help. You must make your claim to the Tribunal within three months of the end of your employment.

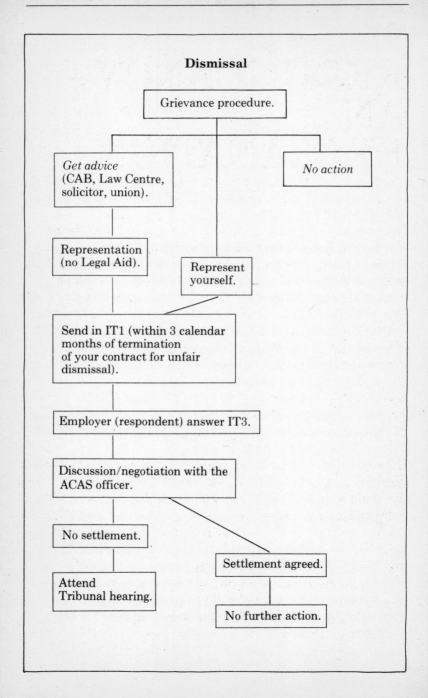

**Dismissal**

Grievance procedure.

*Get advice*
(CAB, Law Centre,
solicitor, union).

*No action*

Representation
(no Legal Aid).

Represent
yourself.

Send in IT1 (within 3 calendar
months of termination
of your contract for unfair
dismissal).

Employer (respondent) answer IT3.

Discussion/negotiation with the
ACAS officer.

No settlement.

Settlement agreed.

Attend
Tribunal hearing.

No further action.

# 8. REDUNDANCY – AN EXPLANATION

When a worker becomes 'surplus to requirement' he or she is said to have become **redundant**. If this position leads to the employee being dismissed or laid-off or put on short-time working, then they may become eligible for a **redundancy payment**. The idea of a redundancy payment is that a worker should be compensated for the loss of their job, so the longer the employment, the higher the amount of redundancy payment to be made. A redundancy payment can be:

1 **Statutory**, which means it is a matter of law.
   **or**
2 **Contractual**, which means it is part of the contract.

The statutory redundancy payments are laid down by the Employment Protection (Consolidation) Act 1978 and are for fixed amounts, but a contractual redundancy payment may be for any amount arranged by your employer as part of your contract. It is more usual for employees to be entitled to the statutory redundancy, but a good many of the larger firms have an amount paid on top of the minimum statutory sum. Sometimes you may be entitled to payment under your employer's contractual redundancy scheme even if you do not qualify for the statutory payment.

## CALCULATING STATUTORY REDUNDANCY PAYMENT

The statutory redundancy payment is calculated as follows:

1   If you are between the ages of 18 and 22 years you will receive half a week's gross pay per year of service.
2   If you are between the ages of 22 and 41 years you will receive one week's gross pay per year of service.
3   If you are between the ages of 41 and 65 (for a man) and 60 (for a woman) you will receive one and half week's gross pay per year of service.

### DO YOU QUALIFY?

In order to qualify for a redundancy payment you must:

1   Be an employee.
2   Have worked continuously in the same employment for two years.
3   Be over the age of 18.
4   Be under retirement age.

If you do not have these qualifications but you are employed you can still be made redundant, but you will not be entitled to any statutory redundancy payment.

### Redundancy and the retirement age

As the law stands a woman's retirement age is 60 and a man's 65, but with the introduction of European law and the Sex Discrimination Act this is changing. Cases have been brought to the courts in which women have claimed the right to go on working until they are 65, and this will be the usual practice in future when the Employment Bill becomes law.

A man also brought an action when he was made to retire early, aged 63. His company pension scheme allowed for a reduced amount to be paid as he was below retirement age. He claimed that he was being discriminated against because of his sex, as a woman who had retired and was aged 63 would be receiving the full entitlement.

In the last year of your employment before your retirement age any redundancy payment which you will get will be reduced by **one-twelfth each month**. This means that if you are made redundant on the day that you retire you will not be entitled to any statutory redundancy payment (although you could be eligible for a contractual payment).

## PEOPLE WHO DO NOT QUALIFY FOR A REDUNDANCY PAYMENT

1 People who are not employed.
2 People over pensionable age.
3 Share fishermen/women paid solely by a share in the catch.
4 Merchant seamen who are covered by redundancy agreements.
5 Crown servants.

## IF YOU ARE NOT PAID YOUR REDUNDANCY PAYMENT

If you are eligible for a payment and your employment does not make redundancy payment, you can take your complaint to an Industrial Tribunal within **six months** of the relevant date, usually when your employment is terminated.

Before actually making such a claim you should write to your employer asking them for the money, and also seek help from the Redundancy Payments Office who may be able to point out your rights to your employer and save you the time and trouble of making a claim. If you have done this, you may make your claim to the Tribunal after the first six months.

## WHAT IS A REDUNDANCY?

There is said to be a redundancy when:

1 Your employer ceases (or intends to cease) trading; in other words if your employer closes his business and there is no job for you to do.
2 Your employer moves (or intends to move) the business to another location. For instance, if they decide to move out of London and into a provincial area, your job in London will become redundant.
3 The need for employees to carry out the work under the contract of employment ceases or diminishes; that is, if your employers decide that they can run the business more efficiently with less employees they will have to choose some people to be made redundant. Under this heading an employer can make people redundant not only because the firm is doing badly but because they decide that it will be more efficient to reduce the workforce.

Normally an employee's job must have disappeared; it is not a redundancy if your employer makes you redundant and then engages someone else to take your place.

Where an employer is making people redundant because they are slimming down the workforce they must not immediately take on new employees. The remaining workers may be moved within the firm to take over the work of the redundant employee, but there must be an overall reduction in the number of people employed.

**If you are made redundant and then replaced**
If your employer makes you redundant and then employs someone else, that will not be a redundancy and you will have been **unfairly dismissed**.

However, when you have been made redundant by your employer, there is no set time before which they can take on another person. This can lead to great difficulties.

Mrs Widdows was a supervisor in a factory making men's trousers. The factory had not been doing very well during the winter and the owner decided that he would make two supervisors redundant and share their duties between himself and the manager. This was done. Mrs Widdows was told that she was to be made redundant, she was offered a job on the factory floor, but she did not want to accept it. She was given proper notice and paid the sum of her redundancy payment.

So far all was well. The owner had behaved perfectly correctly and had paid all that was due to Mrs Widdows.

However, five weeks after being made redundant Mrs Widdows learned that the factory had taken on six more workers and had made up two machinists to be supervisors. Mrs Widdows was very angry and took her case to an Industrial Tribunal, saying that she had not been properly made redundant as she had been replaced some five weeks later.

When the case came to Tribunal, the employer argued that at the time that he dismissed the supervisors there was a redundancy, but four weeks later after those employees' contracts had been terminated, a very large order came into the factory and business doubled almost overnight. In the face of this change the owner and the manager could not cope with doing the work of the supervisors and promoted the machinists and took on extra staff. The Tribunal said that, although it seemed hard that Mrs Widdows had been replaced, there had been no way of knowing at the time that she had been made redundant that there would be further work for her, and her claim failed.

## SELECTION FOR REDUNDANCY

The generally accepted rule for choosing which employee is to be made redundant is **last in, first out**. This means that if you have worked as a driver, for instance, for six months and another driver has worked for your employer for two years, you will be the one who is chosen to be made redundant.

It is generally recognised by the law that employers have a right to run their own business as they choose, but they must behave reasonably to their employees in doing so. If an employer has a criteria or selection method laid down, they must be sure that they follow it when making people redundant. For instance, an employer may want to keep employees with certain skills or qualifications and may decide to make those skills or qualifications that 'test'. If they do apply such tests in the decision where redundancy is concerned they must make sure that they apply the same test to everyone; if they do not, the selection of one employee rather than another may be unfair.

The question of selection for redundancy is a difficult one for an employee to understand, largely because the employer will hold all the information about how and why the choice was made. If you have been made redundant and, for any reason, you think that the choice or circumstances are unfair, in the first instance ask your employer to give you the reasons for the redundancy and the reason why you were chosen to be made redundant. If you are not satisfied, or if there is any difficulty, your local Citizens Advice Bureau or Law Centre may be able to assist you.

## REDUNDANCY – A DISMISSAL

1   When you are made redundant you will be **dismissed**; in other words your contract of employment will be terminated by your employer for reasons for redundancy. This is a fair dismissal.

2   If there is no dismissal, there is no redundancy, and, of course, no redundancy payment. For instance, if you resign, you will not receive a redundancy payment.

3   When you are made redundant you are entitled to **notice** of the termination of your employment in just the same way as you are in other dismissals. If your

employers do not give you notice they must pay you the **money in lieu of notice**.

4　As in any dismissal, you must be given a **date** upon which your contract will come to an end. It is not enough for your employer to say to you 'I will be making you redundant next month'; they must say 'I will be making you redundant and your contract will end on the 25th (or whenever) or next month.' You will then be under notice.

## CONSULTATION

Your employer should consult with you when they are thinking of making you redundant. You should be asked to give your views on the matter and be asked to make suggestions about alternative work that you think you could do. This requirement to consult is obviously a matter of good industrial relations, but many employers take the view that the threat of redundancies can be very disturbing to the workforce. As a result people are often made redundant at very short notice; this practice is often found, for example, in such jobs as sales people, who might upset their employer's customers thereby losing the company business.

Where there is a recognised independent trade union in the business there must be proper consultation with the union representatives at the earliest opportunity. Where an employer is proposing to make 10 or more people redundant they must begin consultation with the union at least 30 days before the dismissals. If you are a member, your union will negotiate with your employer about redundancy or alternative employment on your behalf.

## LOOKING FOR A NEW JOB

When you are under statutory notice of redundancy you have the right to take time off to look for other employment. There is no set amount of time off for this purpose, but up to two days in any one week might be thought reasonable. You should try to cooperate with your employer in the matter of this time off and notify them as far in advance as possible. You should also be prepared to tell them of the time of your interview if you have one, in case it might not be necessary for you to take the whole day off.

## Finding another job while under notice for redundancy

If you are under notice for redundancy and you are successful in finding new employment you may be able to take that employment before your termination date, and still claim your redundancy payment.

In order to leave before your termination date and still be eligible for your redundancy payment, you must be **within your statutory notice period**. For example, if you have worked for a firm for seven years continuously you will be eligible for seven weeks' statutory notice. If your notice period has started, you may be able to leave for another job without losing your redundancy payment. Your employer may not wish to pay you in those circumstances, but an Industrial Tribunal would have to consider all the aspects of your leaving and decide if it was reasonable for you to have left at that time. In most cases you would be awarded all, or the greater part, of your redundancy entitlement.

If you are entitled to contractual notice which is longer than the statutory notice, you must be careful not to take, or propose taking, work before you enter the period of your notice which would amount to the statutory notice. For example:

1 You have worked continuously for your employer for seven years, and you are entitled to three months' contractual notice on the termination of your employment.
2 Your employer has given you three months' notice of redundancy.
3 Your termination date has been given to you.

4   When you are within seven weeks (your statutory notice period) of your termination date you will be entitled to look for other work; if you find such work you may be able to leave and still claim your redundancy payment. You should give your employer notice in writing. If they give you 'counter notice' in writing, saying that they wish you to stay on, then you will be in a difficult position; you will have to decide whether to do as your employer asks, or go against their wishes and risk having an argument over your redundancy payment. It is therefore advisable to keep your present employer informed of developments as you go along.

5   However, if you were to leave before the beginning of your statutory notice period (seven weeks in this case), you would lose your entitlement to a redundancy payment.

## ALTERNATIVE EMPLOYMENT

When your employer is considering making you redundant, he or she must look at the possibility of offering you alternative employment within the firm or with an associate employer.

If you are offered a new job before your contract is terminated, when you are under notice of redundancy, you may be able to refuse it but your refusal must not be unreasonable. In other words, if the job they are offering you is not radically different from your old employment, or if it is reasonable to expect you to be able to do it, then if you do not accept it you will not be eligible for a redundancy payment and the DSS may also consider that you have made yourself intentionally unemployed and stop any unemployment benefit due.

**Is the alternative employment reasonable?**
There are no hard and fast rules about what is a reasonable offer of employment; each case has to be judged on its own merits, and what is reasonable for one

employee may be totally unreasonable for another. If you are offered alternative employment, though, you must consider all sides. You should think of such things as:

1 Can you actually do the work offered?
2 Will you be able to get to the workplace if the hours are different?
3 If the money is reduced, will you be able to manage?
4 Are you willing to accept a drop in status?
5 Are you able to undertake training if it is offered to you?
6 What are your chances of finding other work if you do not accept?

The list is endless and is a matter of personal circumstances. You should therefore think it through carefully and, if necessary, seek advice.

If you think that you might be able to accept the job offered you can have a **trial period of four weeks** in which to make up your mind. You must make it quite clear, in writing, that this is a trial period and if, at any time during those four weeks, you decide that you are unable to accept the job on a permanent basis you may resign and claim your redundancy payment. The trial period can be extended by negotiation between you and your employer, but it should not over-run by too long or your employer may say that you have accepted the alternative employment and you will not be eligible for a redundancy payment.

## WHEN THE BUSINESS IS SOLD – TRANSFER OF UNDERTAKINGS

When a business is sold or is transferred from one employer to another, the contracts of all the employees automatically transfer to the new owner. If the person buying the business does not want all the current employees, he or she may ask that they be made redundant. In this case the redundancy payment would be made by the person selling the business, who is actually making them redundant.

If the business is sold, the new owner takes over and then an employee is made redundant, the normal rules of redundancy apply (alternative employment, selection for redundancy, etc.) and the payments are made by the new employer. However, if the new employer takes on the business and replaces the old employees with new people, they will not be redundant and there might be a claim that they were unfairly dismissed.

The same rules apply on the transfer of an undertaking as in an ordinary redundancy as far as an employee is concerned. There must be a dismissal and that dismissal must be for the reason of redundancy. The sale or transfer of the business does not automatically make anyone redundant.

## WHEN YOUR EMPLOYER CLOSES THE BUSINESS OR GOES BANKRUPT

When your employer cannot afford to make your redundancy payment, it may be that:

1  They are in financial difficulties.
2  They have shut down the business and ceased trading.
3  They are insolvent.

### Employer in financial difficulties

If your employer is in financial difficulties and does not have the money to make redundancy payments to the employees, or, if they did so, they would be putting the future of their business at serious risk, then arrangements can be made for the payments to employees to be issued by the Department of Employment direct from the fund set up for this purpose – the **Redundancy Fund**. You will have to go to an Industrial Tribunal for them to give you a decision saying that you are eligible for a redundancy payment; when you have that, you will be paid from the Fund. Your employer will be expected to pay the money back to the Fund as soon as possible, but you, as an employee, will have received the money due to you as a redundancy payment.

If you have any money in lieu of notice owing to you when your employment is terminated you will have to sue for it; it does not come out of the Redundancy Fund in these circumstances.

## Employer has ceased trading

The same applies when your employer closes the business, but then they will be required to show that there are no assets in the business and that there is genuinely no money to be found.

## Employer is insolvent

In a case where your employer is insolvent, the procedure is slightly different.

If your employer is in financial difficulties and there has been an administration order issued by the court, you should write to the administrator and ask for the payment of your redundancy entitlement out of any remaining funds that are available. The administrator is appointed to look after all the affairs of your employer's business, and you should write to them stating the amount of your claim against your employer. This claim should include claims for such things as:

1  Money in lieu of notice.
2  Holiday pay.
3  Any arrears of wages.

If the company is finally put into liquidation – which means that there is no money left – the receiver will be able to inform the Department of Employment of the employees' redundancies and other payments owing and they will be paid from the Redundancy Fund.

Unfortunately, payment from the Redundancy Fund does take time. If you feel that there has been an unreasonable delay in payment, you should write making your request again. The Department of Employment would then be reminded and should pay more quickly.

If you think that the Department has paid you the wrong amount of money, you can take your complaint to an Industrial Tribunal within three months of the Department's decision to pay. However, you cannot complain to a Tribunal simply because of a delay in the making of the payment to you.

## DEATH OF EMPLOYER OR EMPLOYEE

If your employer was the sole owner of the business, which has ceased to trade as a result of their death, their personal representative will be responsible for your redundancy payment. But if your employer dies and their representative – for instance their husband or wife – carries on the business, then you would not be entitled to a payment as your employment would be continuing.

If an employee dies before receiving a redundancy payment, the payment should be made to their personal representative. The Redundancy Payments Office can give you further information (see addresses, page 143).

# 9.
# LAY-OFF AND SHORT-TIME WORKING

If you are given no work by your employer during a normal working day you may be said to have been laid-off.

If you are laid-off you will **not be paid** by your employer and will be entitled to **unemployment benefit** in the normal way. You may also be entitled to a series of **guarantee payments** (see below).

In most cases a lay-off does not break the contract of employment; it simply interrupts or suspends it until the employer is ready to re-engage or reinstate the employees. Sometimes, though, an employer will decide to lay-off employees hoping that the reduction in their income will force them to leave, thus saving the employer from having to make any redundancy payments.

There is no automatic right in your contract to lay-off, but in certain industries, such as the building industry for instance, there is an implied term that your employer has the right to lay you off if he or she has no work for you to do. In other employments, particularly those covered by union agreements, an employer may have express arrangements about the lay-off of the workers written into the terms and conditions of their employment.

## WHAT ARE LAY-OFFS AND SHORT-TIME WORKING?

### Lay-off
You are said to be laid-off when your employer has no work for you to do under your contract of employment.

This shortage of work can be caused by any number of circumstances, such as:

1 Loss of orders.
2 Financial difficulties.
3 Temporary repairs to the premises.
4 Bad weather making work impossible (particularly in the building industry).

When this situation arises you may be in one of three positions:

1 Your employer may dismiss you, saying that they hope to re-engage you if and when the work picks up or the situation changes. In this case, if you had the required qualifications (see Chapter 8) you would be able to claim a **redundancy payment**, and if you were taken on again it would be under a new contract. If you do not make a claim for redundancy payment at that time and you are re-engaged within a few weeks your contract would still be intact, and it would be considered that there had been no break in your continuous employment.

2 Secondly, your employer may tell you that, for whatever reason, they are going to lay you off. If there is no term in your contract that allows for you to be laid-off, you will be able to claim that you have been **constructively dismissed** (see Chapter 7, page 85).

3 Thirdly, although your employer may not have the right to lay you off, you may decide to accept what has happened and make your own claim for a redundancy under the special provisions of the Act. Again, if your employer is entitled to suspend your contract and lay you off, in those circumstances you are not dismissed; there is no break in the contract and you can either stay on lay-off until your employer calls you back into work, or you can make use of the provisions for claiming redundancy when laid-off under the Act.

## Short-time working

As far as your contract of employment is concerned, short-time working is exactly the same as lay-off. Short-time working is defined as a week in which you receive some pay, but **less than half of your week's pay** in all. You can work, for example, for Monday and Tuesday and be laid-off for Wednesday, Thursday and Friday, and this will count as short-time. But if you work Monday, Tuesday and Wednesday and are only laid off during Thursday and Friday, that would not be counted because you would receive more than half your normal week's pay; it would simply be a temporary cessation of work not affecting your contract.

## Industrial action

You cannot count any week when a lay-off or short-time working was partly or wholly caused by industrial action. Therefore, if you are involved in a strike or a lock-out, that time does not count as lay-off or short-time when you are looking for a possible redundancy claim. It does not matter who causes the strike or lock-out; if it is part of your employment it will not be a proper lay-off and will not count.

## REDUNDANCY PAYMENT AS A RESULT OF LAY-OFF OR SHORT-TIME

The Employment Protection (Consolidation) Act 1978 provides for a claim for a redundancy payment to be made when an employee is laid-off, but the procedure for making such a claim is somewhat complicated. If you are to make a claim when you are laid-off, or on short-time, you must qualify in the following ways:

1  You must have been laid-off or have been on short-time for the right amount of time before making the claim.
2  You must give your employer notice of intention to claim; in other words, you must give them a letter

saying that you are about to make a claim for a
redundancy payment.

3   You must terminate your own contract of
employment. In order to claim a redundancy payment
there has to be a termination of the contract, and in
this situation you, the employee, have to do the
terminating. In practice you must tell your employer
or give them a letter stating that you are giving proper
notice of your resignation; this notice must be one
week, unless the contract calls for more.

4   There must be no possibility of your employer having
work for you in the near future, but this only applies
when your employer has given you counter notice.

## Time limits

Claiming a redundancy payment in these circumstances
depends on **strict time limits**. You must have been
laid-off for:

1   **Four** or more consecutive weeks.
    **or**
2   **Six** or more weeks in any period of **thirteen** weeks
    (but not more than three may be consecutive).

These weeks can be made up of lay-off or short-time, or a
mixture of both.

## How to claim redundancy payments

If you have the right amount of lay-off or short-time you
may start your claim.

1   Your first step is to tell your employer (by letter) that
you **intend** making a claim for a redundancy
payment on the basis that you have been laid-off or on
short-time for the correct period; when you have done
this, you will have made your claim. This in itself does
not get you a payment, but it starts the claim and the
time limits running.

2   When you have given notice of your intention to make

a claim, you have **four weeks** in which to terminate your contract of employment. You can do this by either telling your employer or putting your notice in writing, but you must give at least **one week's notice** (or whatever notice is called for in your contract).

3   At the end of your statutory or contractual notice period you will be entitled to your redundancy payment.

4   If your employer refuses to pay at this point, you have **six months** in which to make a claim to an Industrial Tribunal.

The above is a straightforward claim for a redundancy payment in lay-off.

## Counter-notice

However, it is not always this simple.

If you have given your employer notice of your intention to claim a redundancy payment in writing after the correct period of lay-off, your employer has **seven days** in which to give you counter-notice. Your employer's counter-notice must be in writing, and must state that they reasonably expect that they will be able to start you back at work again within **four weeks** of the date of their counter-notice and that the work is expected to last for **at least thirteen weeks**.

If you have had counter-notice and there is no work forthcoming within four weeks, you will be entitled to take your claim to an Industrial Tribunal for a redundancy payment, but you must terminate your employment with notice within three weeks of the decision of the Tribunal. Then your payment will be due.

If your employer has given you counter-notice, stating that there will be work for you within four weeks of their counter-notice and, while you are in the four-week waiting period, your employer withdraws their counter-notice, you will then have **three weeks from that withdrawal** in which to put in your notice of termination of your employment. Having done that, at the end of your notice period you will be entitled to a redundancy payment from your employer. If they do not make the payment to you when it becomes due, you will have six months in which to make your claim to the Industrial Tribunal.

## Get advice

It is accepted that the provision for claiming a redundancy payment when you are laid-off or on short-time are extremely complicated, so get advice. If your employer tells you that you are to be laid-off you will have to consider all the above possibilities and then act within the strict time-limits. If by any chance you get out of time or make a mistake you may lose your redundancy money. Your local Law Centre or Citizens Advice Bureau will be able to help.

## GUARANTEE PAYMENTS

If you are given no work during your normal working hours, on any day, you may be entitled to a guarantee payment from your employer. The conditions under which you will be entitled to a guarantee payment are:

1   If there is a reduction in the work that you would normally be required to do under your contract.
2   If something else happens (such as extreme weather for instance) which affects your normal working under your contract.

However, in order to qualify for a guarantee payment the following conditions must be satisfied:

1   A payment can only be made for a **complete day** which is lost. A day is defined as 24 hours, from midnight to midnight. Where your contract is for shift work and extends over midnight, the greater number of hours, either before or after midnight, determine which day can be counted as the workless day.

## Lay-off and short-time (time LOST); notice and counter-notice

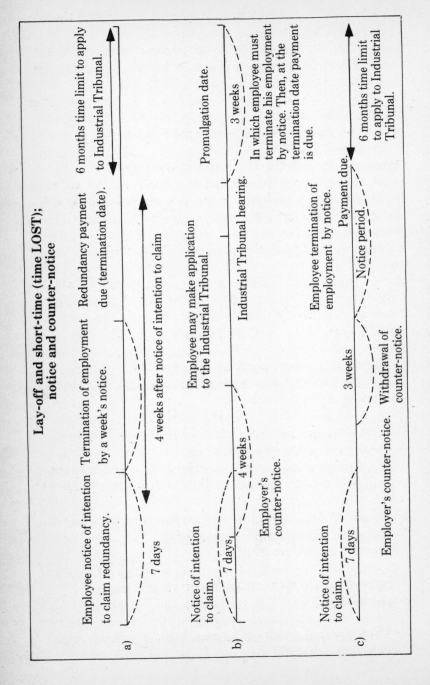

a)
- Employee notice of intention to claim redundancy.
- 7 days
- Termination of employment by a week's notice.
- Redundancy payment due (termination date).
- 4 weeks after notice of intention to claim
- 6 months time limit to apply to Industrial Tribunal.

b)
- Notice of intention to claim.
- 7 days
- 4 weeks
- Employer's counter-notice.
- Employee may make application to the Industrial Tribunal.
- Industrial Tribunal hearing.
- 3 weeks
- Promulgation date.

c)
- Notice of intention to claim.
- 7 days
- Employer's counter-notice.
- Withdrawal of counter-notice.
- 3 weeks
- Notice period.
- Employee termination of employment by notice.
- Payment due.
- In which employee must terminate his employment by notice. Then, at the termination date payment is due.
- 6 months time limit to apply to Industrial Tribunal.

2   You must be **available** for work, even though there is no work for you to do.

3   You must not refuse to do **alternative work** which your employer offers if it is suitable work (see Chapter 8, page 97).

4   If the workless days are caused by your being involved in a strike, lock-out or other **industrial action**, you will not be eligible for a guarantee payment.

In order to claim a guarantee payment from your employer you must have worked continuously for your employer, or an associated employer, for over one month ending with the day for which you intend to claim a guarantee payment.

The amount of the payment is calculated by multiplying your hourly rate of pay by the hours in your normal working day. There is a maximum amount which may be paid as a guarantee payment, this figure being reviewed each year by the Secretary of State for Employment.

## Entitlement to guarantee payments

Your statutory entitlement to guarantee payments in any one period is limited as follows:

1   Five days in any period of three months if you work five or more days a week.

2   If you work for less than five days, your entitlement will be restricted to the number of days that you work under your contract.

3   Where the number of days that you work in a week varies, it is calculated as an average over the last 12 complete working weeks.

## People who do not qualify for guarantee payments

1   People who are not employees, such as independent contractors, etc.

2   Employees who normally work outside Great Britain.
    However most employees working on gas or oil rigs on
    the continental shelf will be included.
3   Employees who normally work less than 16 hours per
    week, unless they work for 8 hours but have been
    continuously employed for more than five years.
4   Employees who have no normal working hours, for
    example insurance agents and certain sales
    representatives.
5   People working in the fishing industry and being paid
    by a share in the profits of the catch.
6   Members of the police force and members of the
    armed forces.

## What to do

If you are laid-off or put on short-time working you should
make a claim for a guarantee payment from your
employer. If you make your claim immediately and it is
found that you do not qualify, it may be that you will be
able to claim other state benefits (such as unemployment
benefit or income support) without delay.

   If your employer refuses to pay you a guarantee
payment to which you are entitled, you can take your
complaint to an Industrial Tribunal, but you must make
your claim within three months of the last day on which
you were due a payment.

# 10. RIGHTS WHEN YOU ARE EXPECTING A BABY, AND AFTER

When you are expecting a baby and are at work, you have four rights:

1 The right to time off for antenatal care, and to be paid while you are taking that time off.
2 The right not to be unfairly dismissed because of your pregnancy.
3 The right to receive maternity pay.
4 The right to return to work after a period of absence on account of pregnancy or confinement.

These rights are generally available to all women, married or unmarried, but they are all, except for the time off for antenatal care, subject to conditions and limitations.

There is not, as yet, a right to paternity leave, as it is called, i.e. there is no statutory right for the father of the child to take time off for the birth or to take time off to look after the baby after it is born. A man may wish to take part of any annual holiday to be present at the birth of a baby or to help look after the baby and the home after the birth, but that is a matter of negotiation with his employer under his contract and not a right under the law. In other parts of the world this right has been awarded to men; for instance, in Hungary either parent can take six months off on full pay, with another year at 75 per cent of full pay, and expect their job to be available to them when they return.

## TIME OFF FOR ANTENATAL CARE

If you are pregnant and are in work, either full- or part-time, you will have the right to paid time off for antenatal care.

Your employer cannot unreasonably refuse you this right, but they can ask you for proof of your pregnancy, such as a certificate from your doctor, midwife or health visitor. You may also be asked for your appointment card or some document about the appointment that has been made for you. You will not need a certificate or document for your first appointment.

You must be paid at your normal hourly rate when you have time off for antenatal care, your hourly rate being calculated by dividing your pay by the number of hours you work, or by averaging your hours in the last 12 weeks. If you have not worked for 12 weeks the figure is arrived at by looking at the hourly rates of other employees.

If your employer refuses to pay you for time off for antenatal care:

1  You should get in touch with your union if you have one.
2  You should contact ACAS, the Advisory, Conciliation and Arbitration Service (see addresses, page 141).
3  Or you can make a complaint to an Industrial Tribunal within three months of the date of your appointment for which payment has been refused and ask the Tribunal to award you the sum that you should have been paid. If you have been paid part of the correct amount, then you can ask for the difference between what you should have been paid and what you were paid. The difficulty with this course of action is that you may risk, at best, your employer's displeasure and, at worse, dismissal.

You can claim time off for antenatal care right from the start of your employment, so if you are pregnant when you start a job you could claim time off straight away.

## ILLNESS WHEN YOU ARE PREGNANT

If you are away from your work because you are sick when you are pregnant it is the same as any other period of sickness, for whatever cause. You will receive sick pay from your employer (either statutory or, where it is part of the contract, contractual sick pay).

However, if you are ill when you are pregnant you should look carefully at the cause of your sickness. There are certain jobs that are dangerous and unsuitable for pregnant women, such as work which involves heavy lifting or work with X-rays.

## HAZARDS AT WORK WHEN YOU ARE PREGNANT

There are special hazards which may be encountered in your employment which might affect your pregnancy, for example:

1   Certain **chemicals** used in manufacturing are considered dangerous to pregnant women. You can obtain a data-sheet from your employer, telling you about what chemicals are being used. If you have difficulty in understanding the data-sheet, consult your union if you have one, or get in touch with your local Health and Safety Inspector and ask them to help.
2   Some conditions in **animals** can affect you when you are pregnant; for instance, spontaneous abortion in sheep can be caught by human beings.
3   There are no legal restrictions on the use of **VDUs** by pregnant women, but there is conflicting evidence as to whether they affect the woman or her child. Trade unions have collected a great deal of evidence on the subject, but as yet there is no definite ruling in law as

to any hazard. The Health and Safety Executive issues a leaflet on the subject, outlining the potential health hazards, which may be of interest for you to read. This leaflet can be obtained at your local Health and Safety Office.

If your work carries risks, or if you think that you might be at risk, consult your trade union or try and talk the matter over with your employer. Seek the support of other employees and try to negotiate with your employer to see if the risk can be avoided.

## DISMISSAL BECAUSE OF PREGNANCY

If you are working in a job that is not suitable for you, your employer can dismiss you from that job, but they must take every effort to offer you **alternative employment**.

If you are offered alternative work you should look very carefully at it and how it will affect you. For example, if there is to be a change in your wages your statutory maternity pay (see below) may be based on your new wages. Again, if you qualify for the right to return to work after your confinement you will need to make it clear that the change in your contract is temporary and that you will expect to return to your own or a very similar job. It is best to get these arrangements put down in writing so that there can be no argument about them at a later date.

### Fair dismissal

If it is illegal for you to continue your work when you are pregnant, or your work is unsuitable because you are pregnant, you can be **fairly dismissed** by your employer. For example, an air-hostess will not be allowed to fly, and if there is no other work for her to do she will be considered to have been fairly dismissed. If this happens you may keep your statutory rights, although you will have no continuing contract of employment. If you are fairly dismissed in these circumstances you will still be entitled to statutory maternity pay (see below).

If you are dismissed before the 11th week before the expected date of your confinement and, had you not been dismissed you would have completed two years continuous employment by the 11th week, you will still keep your right to return to work, provided you follow the proper procedure (see below).

## Unfair dismissal

If you have been employed:

1   Continuously for two years working for 16 hours per week
    **or**
2   Continuously for five years working for eight hours per week

and you are dismissed by your employer, you will have the right to claim unfair dismissal if you are dismissed for any of the following:

1   If you are dismissed simply because you are pregnant.
2   If your dismissal is for a fair reason, but your employer fails to offer you suitable alternative employment.
3   If your employer refuses to allow you to return to work after your confinement (to your own or a similar job).
4   If you are selected for redundancy because you are pregnant.

You can make a complaint to an Industrial Tribunal, but your claim must be made within three months of your dismissal or of the date on which you would have returned to your job.

## SEX DISCRIMINATION AND PREGNANCY

If because of your pregnancy, your employer treats you less favourably than a man would be treated, you may be able to claim that you have been discriminated against because of your sex. To be able to claim unfair dismissal because of pregnancy you will have to have had two years' continuous service. However you can make a claim under the Sex Discrimination Act that your treatment has been less favourable than that of a man, without the length of service requirement.

There have been several women who have successfully claimed that they have been discriminated against because they were pregnant. For instance:

Mrs Fife was a part-time baker employed to prepare pastry and to line quiche tins. She also had to do other jobs such as loading tins into the ovens and removing them, which involved a certain amount of lifting. When she had been working for her employer for six months, Mrs Fife went off sick because she was suffering from 'excessive vomiting'. After a continuous absence of two months, her employer dismissed her because of her pregnancy.

Mrs Fife argued that the firm had employed a van driver who had been away sick because he had pulled some ligaments in his shoulder and was unable to drive – he was away for two months and was not dismissed. In fact, the employer found a temporary replacement to do the job until such time as he would be able to return to work. It was found that Mrs Fife had been treated less favourably than the male employee, the only explanation of this treatment being that Mrs Fife was female and pregnant. Mrs Fife was awarded £570 to cover loss of earnings and sick pay, and £500 for injury to her feelings.

## REDUCTION IN WORKING HOURS BECAUSE OF PREGNANCY

You may find that you are increasingly tired and stressed at work due to your pregnancy, and may wish to have a reduction in your working hours for a period before you commence your maternity leave. There is no statutory right for you to be able to change your contract in this way, but you may be able to negotiate with your employer and he or she may allow you to work part-time or at reduced hours by agreement.

You should consider the consequences of such an arrangement very carefully because:

1   If your hours are reduced it could affect your statutory maternity pay (see below).
2   If you are unfairly dismissed during that period it could affect the amount of compensation which you would be awarded.
3   If you wish to return to work after the baby, you will only be entitled to return to the conditions which were in force when you started your maternity leave.
4   If your hours are reduced below 16 per week and you have not worked for more than two years, you will not be entitled to claim unfair dismissal and your right to return to work will be affected.
5   If your hours are reduced to below eight per week you will have to have worked for five years to be able to claim unfair dismissal and the right to return to work after the birth.
6   If your hours are reduced to below eight per week you will lose all your statutory rights that are based on continuous employment.
7   If you are working part-time your national insurance record and contractual rights, such as holidays, may be affected.
8   Often part-time workers find themselves working more hours than they planned.

## THE RIGHT TO RETURN TO WORK AFTER HAVING A BABY

In order to qualify for your rights under the EP(C)A – the right not to be unfairly dismissed because of your

pregnancy and the right to return to work – you must
have been continuously employed for:

1   16 hours or more per week for two years
    **or**
2   8 hours or between 8 and 16 hours per week for five
    years **before the 11th week** before the expected
    week of confinement.

The law says that if you have the required length of
service you will have the right to have your own, or a
similar, job back and your contract will be preserved for
the purposes of calculating continuous employment. In
other words, your contract will not be broken by your
being absent through maternity leave. There are strict
rules about claiming your right to return to work which
you must follow, otherwise your employer can say that the
contract has been terminated.

## Exceptions

If your employer has five or less employers you will not
have the statutory right to return to either your own or
suitable alternative employment if your employer says
that it is not reasonably practicable to have you back.
However, you may have contractual rights, or be able to
negotiate your return with your employer.

## Suitable alternative employment

You have the right to return to your own job, but your
employer may decide to offer you alternative employment
when you return. This alternative work must be suitable
for you to do and you should consider it carefully in the
light of such things as:

1   Will you be more at risk of redundancy?
2   Will it be of lower status, which may affect future
    promotion?
3   Will it have less pay, overtime, etc.?

All these considerations should be looked at before you make up your mind. If the job offered to you is not suitable you can complain to an Industrial Tribunal within three months of the date on which you would have started the job.

## Preserving your right to return to work

1 You must have been employed continuously for **two years** and be working immediately **before the 11th week** before the expected week of confinement.
2 You must inform your employers that you intend to begin your maternity leave **21 days** before your leave starts (or, if that is not possible, as near as is practicable after that 21 days).
3 You must give this **notice in writing** before you actually stop work, stating:
   - You will be absent because of your pregnancy.
   - The date your baby is expected.
   - That you intend to return after your confinement.
4 Even if you have not decided whether you will return after having your baby, you should claim your right to return by putting it in writing before you start your maternity leave. If you do not you **cannot claim it at a later date**.
5 If you have claimed your right to return to work in this way – it is not binding – you can change your mind later on.
6 Your employer is entitled to ask you for medical evidence as to your pregnancy and the expected date of your confinement. If asked, you should give them a copy of the medical certificate from your doctor or midwife.
7 Your employer can ask you to confirm that you wish to return to work after the birth, but this request must not be made **before 49 days** after the expected week of confinement. If your employer makes this request you must reply in **writing** within 14 days of receiving the letter (or as soon after as is reasonably practicable)

or you will lose your right to return. However, your employer must warn you in his letter of the need for you to reply within 14 days.

8 If you decide to return to work you can do so at any time up to 29 weeks after the actual confinement.

9 You must give your employer 21 days notice in writing that you intend to return to work. In that letter you must give your employer **the date** on which you will be returning.

10 Your employer can decide to **extend** your maternity leave for up to **four weeks** after you have given them your return date, but they must give you the reason in writing. You can only extend your leave beyond that date with a doctor's certificate.

11 You may have a contractual right to a longer maternity absence and those rights may include a different length of notice. For example, if you were entitled to one year off, you might be asked to give three months notice of your return rather than the 21 days. If you have contractual maternity arrangements these will apply even if you do not have enough service for the statutory rights.

You may not wish to go back to the work that you were doing before your confinement but would prefer to work part-time. You have no statutory right to change your contract, but you may be able to negotiate with your employer. If you are a member of a trade union your shop steward should be asked to help.

You may be able to negotiate a phased return, starting part-time and going on to full-time later. You may like to contact the Working Mothers Association for advice (see addresses, page 144).

## MATERNITY LEAVE

You are required to give your employer 21 days notice of your intention to start your maternity leave. If you do not do so, your employer can insist that your leave starts at a later date.

If you have not given the 21 days notice to your employer, you must give them the reason for the delay. Such things as illness, lost in the post, lost in the employer's internal post system, and so on might be considered as being reasonable excuses, but in the end it is up to your employer to decide.

If you stop working without agreement you can be **fairly dismissed**, or you may lose some of your statutory maternity rights under your contract.

## PAYMENTS DURING MATERNITY LEAVE

A woman who is absent through pregnancy and confinement may be entitled to:

1  Contractual maternity pay.
2  Statutory maternity pay.
3  Maternity allowance.

### Contractual maternity pay

Your contract may provide for maternity pay for an extended period, for instance for three months on full pay, plus three months on half pay. Contractual maternity pay is usually paid in the form of wages with deductions for tax, national insurance, etc. You are unlikely to get full pay plus your statutory maternity pay or maternity allowance, but proportions of pay might be paid. It will depend on your contract.

If you are entitled to statutory maternity pay and/or contractual maternity pay you will receive tax refunds through the PAYE system when the amount of your income drops.

### Statutory maternity pay

The main features of statutory maternity pay (SMP) are as follows:

1   SMP is a payment **from your employer** which will be paid when you have time off to have a baby.
2   It is paid for up to 18 weeks – this is called your **maternity pay period**.
3   SMP can be paid **after the 11th week** before your baby is due, but in order to get the full amount you must start claiming not later than six weeks before your baby is due.
4   SMP is paid at **two rates**, depending on how long you have worked and how you have been paid. There are no increases for dependents.
5   Your employer will make **deductions** for tax, national insurance, union dues, etc., from your SMP in the same way as he or she does for your ordinary pay.
6   You can claim income support (if you are eligible) while you are receiving SMP, but the figure of your SMP will be taken into account.
7   You will *not* be able to get maternity allowance, sickness benefit, statutory sick pay or invalidity benefit when you are receiving SMP.

*Eligibility*   In order to qualify for SMP you must have worked continuously in your job for six months up to and including the **qualifying week**, which is 15 weeks before the baby is due, i.e. the 26th week of pregnancy.

You will not qualify for SMP if you do not work into the qualifying week. However, if you are fairly dismissed by your employer before the qualifying week (because it might be hazardour for you to continue working, for instance) you may be able to qualify.

You will definitely not qualify for SMP if you are:

1   Not an employee.
2   Solely self-employed.
3   A member of HM forces.
4   Working for an employer who has no place of business in the UK.

5     Taken into legal custody (your SMP will stop if you
      are taken into legal custody while it is being paid).

*How to get your SMP*   If you are pregnant and are eligible
for SMP you must give your employer 21 days notice that
you intend to stop work to have your baby. If it is not
possible to give 21 days, you must give it as soon as
possible. You may be asked to give this notice in writing,
and you should include in it notice that you intend to
return to work after having your baby.
   If your baby is born prematurely, you may still be able
to get SMP (see below).
   You must give your employer proof that you are
pregnant. This can be done by giving them a maternity
certificate (**MAT B1**) which you can get from your
doctor or midwife. Your cannot get a MAT B1 until you
reach the 14th week before your baby is due, and you
should give your employer the medical evidence no later
than three weeks after the date on which the SMP was
due to start (see Maternity Leave, page 120).

*Payment of SMP*   There are two rates at which SMP is
paid:

1     The **lower rate** – this will be paid for 18 weeks, with
      no increases for dependents.
2     The **higher rate** – this rate is 90 per cent of your
      gross weekly earnings and is paid for the first six
      weeks of your maternity period. This is followed by 12
      weeks at the lower rate.

The amount of SMP that you are paid is based on the
actual money that you receive on:

1     Your last eight pay-days before the qualifying date, if
      you are paid weekly.
2     If you have more than one pay-day per week all your
      pay-days in the last eight weeks will count.
3     If you are paid monthly your weekly pay will be

averaged out over the year and reduced to the relevant period of eight weeks before your qualifying date.

The calculation is made on your **actual** pay. It will not matter that you have earned extra pay in bonus or overtime in the period, or that you are on statutory sick pay during that time – though of course this will affect the amount you will receive in SMP.

Your SMP should be paid in the normal way that your wages are paid; if you are paid weekly then you should receive your SMP weekly, and if you are paid monthly then your SMP should be paid to you monthly. Your employer will deduct tax and national insurance from your SMP in the normal way.

Your contract may entitle you to paid maternity leave at a rate that is more or less than SMP. However if you qualify for SMP your employer cannot pay you less than the SMP rate that you are entitled to receive.

*Premature births and SMP*   If your baby is born prematurely, it may not affect your SMP:

1   If your baby is born after the start of your maternity pay period your SMP will not be affected.
2   If your baby is born before your maternity pay period has started but after the qualifying week you must (if reasonably practicable) inform your employer of the birth within three weeks.
3   If your baby is born within the qualifying week you must inform your employer (if reasonably practicable) within three weeks of the birth. You will then be taken to have been continuously employed for the purposes of your SMP and the payment period will run from the week in which your baby was born.
4   If your baby is born before you have given your employer notice that you intend to stop work to have a baby, you must supply your evidence of the birth (the birth certificate will do) within three weeks. Then your maternity pay period will be 18 weeks from the date of the birth.

*Twins or multiple birth and SMP*   If you expecting twins or more than one baby you will only be entitled to one amount of SMP.

*Stillbirths and miscarriages and SMP*   If your baby is born earlier than the 29th week of your pregnancy you will not be able to get SMP, although you may be able to get **statutory sick pay**. You should talk to your employer and seek their help.

If your baby is stillborn after the start of the 29th week of your pregnancy you will be entitled to the same amount of SMP as you would have been had the baby been born alive. In these circumstances you will also keep your right to return to work in the usual way. Contractual maternity rights may not apply when there is a stillbirth, but you can insist on receiving any statutory rights to which you are entitled.

## Maternity allowance

Maternity allowance is a benefit paid by the DSS to some pregnant women who do not qualify for SMP. You can only get it if you **do not get SMP or unemployment benefit**. To qualify for maternity allowance you must have been employed or self-employed and paying the standard rate NI contributions for at least 26 weeks in the 52-week period ending with the 15th week before the baby is due.

1   The same rules apply for maternity allowance as SMP for premature births, twins or multiple births and for stillbirths.
2   You may be able to claim an extra sum for an adult dependent while you are claiming maternity allowance.
3   You cannot get SSP or unemployment benefit if you are being paid maternity allowance.
4   If you do not qualify for maternity allowance or SMP, you may be able to get sickness benefit for the period

starting six weeks before the baby is due to 14 days after the birth.

5   If you are claiming unemployment benefit and do not qualify for maternity allowance, you may be able to go on claiming for a time but you will have to be available for and capable of work.

## CONCLUSION

As the rules during maternity relating to your right to return to work and to claim SMP or maternity allowance are very complicated, you should consult the DSS or your Citizens Advice Bureau at the start of your pregnancy, so that you can be sure of being given your rights when the time comes.

Note the two **essential dates:**

1   The 11th week before the baby is due, for the right to return to work and when SMP begins to be paid.
2   The 15th-week-before-the-baby-is-due qualification for maternity allowance, although payment will only start after the 11th week.

# 11.
# INDUSTRIAL TRIBUNALS AND HOW THEY WORK

The Industrial Tribunals were set up in 1964 with the idea that they would be industrial courts which would deal swiftly and informally with employment disputes. In practice they have become highly formal affairs with complex and technical procedures which can be very daunting to the inexperienced. In one way an Industrial Tribunal can appear informal because the people taking part are not judges – they do not dress up in wigs and gowns, the 'court' is an ordinary room (often a room in a commercial building that has been hired by the Regional Office of Industrial Tribunals for the day or week) which has ordinary tables and chairs, nobody addresses anyone as 'M'lud' or 'your worship' and, usually, everyone at the hearing remains seated throughout the proceedings.

On the other hand, if you have never been involved in legal proceedings before you may find the whole thing rather overwhelming because, in spite of the original intention, the hearing is complicated. For instance:

1 Evidence is given on oath (or affirmation if appropriate).
2 You and your witnesses will be cross-examined by the representative on the other side.
3 You, or your representative if you have one, will be invited to cross-examine the witnesses put up by the respondents (your employers).
4 Legal submissions are presented.

In other words, the way the hearing is conducted follows exactly the same procedure as any other court and you will be expected to attend appropriately dressed (in your 'best', not your 'working' clothes).

## LEGAL AID FOR REPRESENTATION AT TRIBUNAL

Although you may feel that you need help in presenting your case to the Tribunal you cannot get legal aid for representation at the Industrial Tribunal.

If you are on a low income, out of work or in receipt of state benefits, and your savings are below a certain figure, you may be eligible for legal advice which will help you to prepare your case. However, unless you can pay a solicitor, find a Citizens Advice Bureau that provides representation, or a Law Centre or free representation unit that can help, you will be on your own. If you are representing yourself at a Tribunal you will find that the chairman (see Chapter 12, page 136) will try to be as helpful as he can, but he cannot advise you on the conduct of your case and how you decide to present your evidence.

The majority of employers – called the respondents – employ solicitors to represent them and occasionally a solicitor will brief a barrister, all of which does not lend itself to informality.

## DECIDING TO TAKE YOUR CASE TO A TRIBUNAL

Although you may feel very aggrieved about how your contract has been terminated or how your employer is behaving towards you, it may not always mean that you have a good enough case to take to a Tribunal. The decision is yours, but do get advice in some form or other before you make up your mind. It is often easier for another person, who is not so close to the problem, to take a more balanced view of the situation.

## Getting advice

1   If you are a member of a union get in touch with the branch secretary or paid official who will be able to advise.
2   If you are not a member of a union, ask your local Citizens Advice Bureau if they can help.
3   Ask your Citizens Advice Bureau if they can recommend a solicitor who specialises in employment law, although you must remember that you will have to pay him or her to represent you.
4   Find the address of your local Law Centre and see what they advise.

When you go to see anyone to seek their advice on your claim take **all the paperwork** with you. They will need to see such things as your terms and conditions of employment if you have them, any letter of appointment, any written warnings (or commendations) if you have had them, your dismissal letter if you have been given one and anything to do with your employment as a whole. This will enable your adviser to form a full picture of your case and give you the best advice on whether or not to proceed.

The decision is finally yours, but seek and listen to the best advice in order to make your decision.

## TIME LIMITS

There are strict time limits for making a claim to an Industrial Tribunal, and you must be very careful not to miss them.

1   If you are making a claim for **unfair dismissal** you have **three months from the date of the termination of your employment** in which to register your claim by sending your application to the Central Office of Industrial Tribunals in London (see addresses, page 141).
2   If you are claiming a **redundancy payment** you have **six months from your termination date**.

**Time limits for application to Industrial Tribunal**

| Claim | Time limit | From |
|---|---|---|
| Unfair dismissal Itemised pay statements Written reasons for dismissal | Three months | From termination date |
| Maternity pay | Three months | From the last day of payment |
| Guarantee payment | Three months | From date upon which payment is refused |
| Redundancy payment | Six months | From termination date |
| Dismissal for trade union activities | Three months | From dismissal or act complained of |
| Sex discrimination claim | Three months | From the date when the discrimination took place |
| Race discrimination claim | Three months | From the date when the discrimination took place |
| Claim under the Wages Act | Three months | From the deduction or non-payment complained of |
| Equal pay and equal value claims | No time limit | |

The Department of Employment leaflets on the subject of making an application to an Industrial Tribunal say that you must get your claim in within three months; if it is received any later the Tribunal will consider whether it was 'reasonably practicable' for you to have got it in in time. In practice there are very few examples of a case being heard if the application is made out of time, although very serious illness and admission to hospital might qualify, or a genuine lack of knowledge that you actually had a potential claim and had received no advice from any source which could have led you to believe that you had a claim. The arguments when there is an application presented out of time are complicated and very seldom successful.

You must therefore always be aware of the time limit for your claim, even if you are in the process of writing to your employer for written reasons for your dismissal (see Chapter 5, page 58) and waiting for a reply. If the end of the three months is approaching you must get your application in without delay (see chart opposite).

## THE GRIEVANCE PROCEDURE – HAVE YOU USED IT?

You, as an employee, must be seen to be a 'reasonable employee', just as your employer should be a 'reasonable employer'. When there is a problem in your employment, or if you have been dismissed, in most circumstances you should be thinking about protesting or appealing against what has happened – in other words using your employer's agreed grievance procedure.

If you have written terms and conditions of your employment you will find your employer's grievance procedure set out. Following this procedure should therefore be straightforward.

If you do not have such a procedure in writing, you should appeal to your immediate superior or someone in authority higher up. Your appeal should be in writing and you should keep a copy of your letter in case your appeal fails and you have to go to an Industrial Tribunal. If you are working for a very small firm where you and your boss work together on a daily basis, it will be more difficult for you to appeal. Probably in these circumstances the person to whom you would have to appeal will be the person who dismissed you or upset your contract in the first place. However, you should still try to appeal to them to change their mind or discuss the changes, because the very act of appealing may bring your grievance out into the open and the matter might be settled.

While you are making your appeals and using the grievance procedure remember the Industrial Tribunal time limits – you cannot argue you got out of time because you were hoping to settle without having to go to the Tribunal. Enter the application and tell the Tribunal that you are in the process of using the grievance procedure and, should it be settled, you will withdraw your application.

Do not miss the deadline.

## MAKING A CLAIM TO AN INDUSTRIAL TRIBUNAL

When you have decided that you wish to make a claim to an Industrial Tribunal you must send your application for a hearing to the Central Office of Industrial Tribunals (see addresses, page 141) within three months of the effective date of the termination of your employment. Your application can, in theory, be in the form of a letter containing:

1   Your name and address.
2   Your employer's name and address.
3   The nature of your claim.
4   The grounds (reasons) for your claim.

**The form you fill in**

It is more usual to send the application on a form which you will get from a Jobcentre, some unemployment benefit offices, some Citizens Advice Bureaux and Law Centres. This form is called the **IT1**, the initiating application to the Industrial Tribunal (see specimen forms, page 159). It is fairly easy to fill in, but if you are in any doubt seek help.

The information for which you are asked on the 1T1 is pretty straightforward. Apart from your personal particulars you must give:

1   The **name and address of your employer**. Be careful that you get the right name; for example 'Mr John Brown, of Messrs William Smith' will not do – Mr John Brown may only be your manager and not the company that employs you. You may put William Smith as your employer, or William Smith & Co., but William Smith is not the same as William Smith Ltd. So make sure that you get it right. It may help to look

at any paperwork that you have received in the past from your employer, such as letters, etc. – the name should be printed on these.

2    The **title of the job** that you did. This means the job that you were doing just before the end of your employment, not the job you originally did when you started.

3    Your **pay details**. Give your basic gross weekly earnings and your weekly net pay – the latter figure should include any overtime or bonus that you earn. If your earnings vary from week to week, you should average them out over the 12 weeks before the termination date to arrive at your net figure.

4    Any **fringe benefits** you get under your contract such as company car, canteen meals, loan facilities, accommodation, private pension, medical insurance, etc. These things will all be part of your loss when you have been dismissed.

5    At paragraph 10 you are asked to give your grounds or **reasons for your claim**. You should keep this as short as you can because you will be able to fill in the details when you get to the hearing.

## What you can get at a Tribunal

Finally you have to decide what remedy you want if you win your case. There are three choices:

1    You can ask to be **reinstated in your job**. This means that you will get your old job back again.

2    You can ask for **re-engagement**. In this case you will be taken back to work by your employer, but under a new contract, probably doing different work.

3    You can ask for **compensation**. This is a monetary award to compensate you for the loss of your job.

There is, at present, no charge for having your case heard by an Industrial Tribunal, but a clause in the Employment Bill states that a deposit of up to £150 can be demanded if it is thought that your case is not of a serious nature and will waste the Tribunal's time. This

order for the payment of a deposit will only be made after
your case has been considered at a special hearing called
a 'Pre-hearing Review'. In the ordinary way, your
application will go through and there will be no charge or
deposit as before.

*Compensation*   The amount you will be awarded if you
win your case at an Industrial Tribunal is often quite
small. The Tribunal awards are made up as follows:

1   The **basic award**. This figure is the same as the
statutory redundancy figure (see Chapter 8, page 90).

2   The **compensatory award**, made up of the actual
loss that you will have suffered through being made
unemployed. It will be the amount you are paid after
deductions have been made for tax and national
insurance contributions by your employer. The figure
will include the value of any fringe benefits to which
you were entitled under your contract, such as
pension, company car, canteen meals, etc.

3   **Future loss**. This is the same figure as the actual
loss, but it applies to the future loss you will continue
to have after the date of the Tribunal hearing. The
length of time for calculation of this loss will depend
on the possibility of your getting a new job if you
haven't got one, or the chance of your getting
promotion if you are in work.

4   **Loss of statutory rights**. This is a small figure, to
compensate you for the loss of your right to claim
unfair dismissal, etc., in your new employment for two
years.

5   **Job search expenses**. You may claim from your
ex-employer any expenses you have incurred in
looking for work, such as telephone calls, postage, bus
fares, petrol, etc. You must have kept a record of these
for the Tribunal to look at at the hearing.

Any unemployment benefit or income support which you
have been paid since you became unemployed will be
deducted from the award and, if you have found another
job at lower wages, anything you have earned will further
reduce your award.

If you have found work in which you are earning more than your original job, you will not be awarded compensation as you will have sustained no loss. You will only be entitled to the basic award for the loss of your job.

There is a maximum figure for an award at an Industrial Tribunal which is increased from time to time.

## What you can't get at an Industrial Tribunal

Although you can get compensation for the loss of your job in the basic award and compensation for your loss of earnings and fringe benefits, you cannot get compensation for loss of dignity or hurt feelings. The compensation figures are regulated by law, and although there is a certain amount of room for discussion on such things as overtime and fringe benefits, the calculation of the actual loss is fairly strict.

## ACAS – WHAT THEY DO AND HOW THEY CAN HELP

ACAS, the **Advisory, Conciliation and Arbitration Service**, have a very important part to play in Industrial Tribunal claims.

When you send in your application to the Central Office of Industrial Tribunals, a copy of it is sent to your employer for them to answer and put their side of the case. Copies of both your application and your employer's answer (their notice of appearance) are sent to ACAS so that a conciliation officer can try to help the parties make a settlement without going to Tribunal. The ACAS officer does not tell you what you should do, but they can help you decide whether a settlement of your claim is possible. The ACAS officer is not on your side, neither are they on the side of the respondents (your employer): they are impartial. Above all the ACAS service is confidential.

If you agree to a settlement through ACAS they can draw up an agreement for you to sign which will bind you and the respondents to what is agreed. When you have told the ACAS officer that you agree to settle, you cannot change your mind – it is a legal agreement.

# 12.
# THE ACTUAL TRIBUNAL

## WHO SITS ON INDUSTRIAL TRIBUNALS?

An Industrial Tribunal is made up of three people:

1   The **Chairman** – not 'chair-person', although women frequently hold the post (they are addressed as 'Madam Chairman'). They must be a barrister or solicitor of at least seven years' standing.
2   A **member of the Confederation of British Industries** (CBI) who brings the experience of management to the Tribunal decision-making.
3   An **official of a trade union** who can advise the Tribunal on industrial affairs.

Members of Industrial Tribunals are appointed by the Lord Chancellor and the proceedings are governed by statute. The mixture of a legal chairman and lay people to help them is a deliberate attempt to bring common sense into the decisions of the Tribunals.

## WHAT HAPPENS AT A TRIBUNAL

There is a set formula when you go to an Industrial Tribunal, although the chairman can decide to alter it if necessary.

1   If you have been dismissed, your employer will have to put his or her case first.
2   If dismissal is denied (see Chapter 7, Constructive dismissal, page 85) you will have to put your case first.

3  If your employer is represented by a solicitor, he or she will make a short introductory speech about the business and the people who work for it and then put the witnesses through their evidence.

4  The clerk to the Tribunal will administer the oath to the witnesses and then they will give their evidence, one by one. After each witness finishes, you will have a chance to cross-examine them about what they have said.

5  The Tribunal themselves will ask witnesses questions as the case goes along. When all the employer's witnesses have finished giving evidence you will have your chance.

6  If you are represented, the person who is representing you will help you to give your side of the argument to the Tribunal. You will be cross-examined by the other side, and the Tribunal may put questions to you.

7  When your evidence is complete and your witnesses (if any) have had their say and have been cross-examined, you (or your representative) will be able to make your submissions. This means that you will have a chance to sum up your case as you see it and, if possible, to quote any other cases that have been decided in higher courts that you can use as a comparison.

8  When you have finished, it will be the turn of the respondents or their representatives to sum up in the same way.

9  When all the evidence has been given, the submissions have been made and the case is completed, the Tribunal will consider all the evidence that has been given and come to a conclusion one way or the other and give their decision.

## THE DECISION

The decision of an Industrial Tribunal can be in one of three forms:

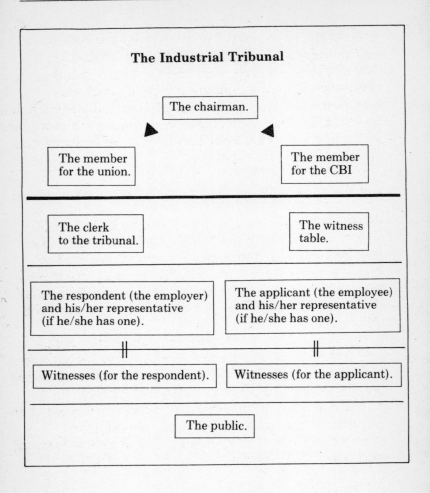

**The Industrial Tribunal**

The chairman.

The member for the union.

The member for the CBI

The clerk to the tribunal.

The witness table.

The respondent (the employer) and his/her representative (if he/she has one).

The applicant (the employee) and his/her representative (if he/she has one).

Witnesses (for the respondent).

Witnesses (for the applicant).

The public.

1  You **succeed** – you win your case.
2  You **fail** – you lose your case.
3  You succeed, but you are awarded **contributory fault**. This means that the Tribunal consider that although it was unfair for the employer to dismiss you, you behaved in some way which contributed to your dismissal. If the Tribunal comes to this decision, your compensation will be reduced by a percentage, the amount of the reduction being decided by the Tribunal.

In most instances the decision of the Tribunal will be given to you at the end of your case and you will receive a written copy at a later date.

If you have won your case and have been awarded compensation or a redundancy payment and your employer does not pay, you can automatically enforce the award in the county court. You can find out the procedure for enforcing an Industrial Tribunal award by contacting your local county court office.

## COSTS AND EXPENSES

Normally there are no costs awarded by an Industrial Tribunal. However if the Tribunal consider that a case has been conducted improperly or that there has been undue delay in some form, they will award costs against the person concerned. These will not include the costs of the other side's case, but will be a figure decided by the Tribunal.

If you have decided to instruct a solicitor to represent you at the Tribunal you must expect to pay his bill, even if you have lost your case. There is no legal aid or monetary help for representation at Industrial Tribunals.

You can claim certain expenses when you appear at an Industrial Tribunal, whether you are making the application yourself or appearing as a witness in someone else's case. For example:

1   Travelling expenses.
2   Meals allowance.
3   Loss of earnings.
4   Interpreter's fees.
5   Allowance for staying overnight.

All these things are paid at a set rate. You should ask the clerk to the Tribunal to give you a form and a list of the things that you may claim.

## APPEALING AGAINST THE DECISION OF AN INDUSTRIAL TRIBUNAL

You can only appeal against the decision of an Industrial Tribunal on a **point of law**. This is a very complex matter and well beyond the scope of this book.

When you receive the decision of the Tribunal you will find a date stamped on the final page, next to the signature of the chairman. You will have **42 days from that date** in which to lodge your appeal to the **Employment Appeal Tribunal**, which is the court above the Industrial Tribunal. If you think that there might be good reason for you to make an appeal against the decision, you should seek advice without delay.

If you are eligible you will be able to get legal aid for an appeal to the Employment Appeal Tribunal. You should consult a solicitor as soon as possible after you receive the decision, as there will be much to do. If you have not had a solicitor to help you with the Tribunal you can ask the Citizens Advice Bureau or local Law Centre to help you find one who will take your case to appeal.

You cannot appeal against the decision simply because you do not like what has been decided. It must be on a point of law. **Seek advice**.

# USEFUL ADDRESSES

**Advisory, Conciliation and Arbitration Service (ACAS)**
87 Wilton Street
London SW1X 7AZ
01-210 3600

**Central Office of Industrial Tribunals (COIT)**
93 Ebury Bridge Road
London SW1W 8RE
01-730 9161

Write to the Secretary of the Tribunals. This office deals with England and Wales. The address for Northern Ireland is:
**Northern Ireland Central Office of Industrial Tribunals (COIT)**
2nd Floor
Bedford House
16 Bedford Street
Belfast BT2 7NR
0232 327666

**Commission for Racial Equality**
Eliot House
10–12 Allington Street
London SW1E 5EH
01-828 7022

**Employment Appeal Tribunal**
*Central Office:*
4 St James' Square
London SW1Y 4JU
01-210 3000

*Divisional Office:*
11 Melville Crescent
Edinburgh EH3 7LU
031-225 3963

**Equal Opportunities Commission (EOC)**
Overseas House
Quay Street
Manchester M3 3HN
061-833 9244

The EOC also has regional offices in **Wales**:
Equal Opportunities Commission
Caerwys House
Windsor Lane
Cardiff CF1 1LB
0222 43552

in **Scotland**:
Equal Opportunities Commission
St Andrews House
141 West Nile Street
Glasgow G1 2RU
041-332 8018

and in **Northern Ireland**:
Equal Opportunities Commission
Lindsay House
Callender Street
Belfast BT71 5DT
0232 242752

**Irish Congress of the TUC**: Northern Ireland
Committee
3 Wellington Park
Belfast BT9 6DJ
0232 681726

## Law Centres Confederation
Duchess House
18–19 Warren Street
London W1P 5DB
01-387 8570

## Law Society
113 Chancery Lane
London WC2
01-242 1222

## National Association of Citizens Advice Bureaux (NACAB)
Myddleton House
115–17 Pentonville Road
London N1 9LZ
01-833 2181

## Redundancy Payments Office
The Department of Employment has regional offices
covering different parts of the country. Contact your local
Jobcentre or benefit office to find the address which will
apply to you.

## Scottish Central Office of Industrial Tribunals (SCOIT)
St Andrews House
141 West Nile Street
Glasgow G1 2RU
041-331 1601

## Scottish TUC
16 Woodlands Terrace
Glasgow G3 6DF
041-332 4946

## Trades Union Congress (TUC)
Great Russell Street
London WC1B 3LS
01-636 4030

## Wages Inspectorate
Clifton House
83–117 Euston Road
London NW1 2RB
01-387 2511

## Women's Legal Defence Fund
29 Great James Street
London WC1N 3ES
01-831 6890

## Working Mothers' Association
23 Webbs Road
London SW11 6RU
01-228 3757

# FURTHER
# READING

*Harvey on Industrial Relations and Employment Law,*
(Available in most public libraries. Regularly updated,
Butterworths, London)

*I D S Brief Employment Law and Practice* and *I D S
Employment Law Handbooks,* Incomes Data Services Ltd,
193 St John's Street, London EC1V 4LS, 071 250 3434.

Smith and Wood *Industrial Law,* Butterworths, London,
EC1V 4LS, 1983.

Cyril Grunfeld *The Law of Redundancy* Sweet & Maxwell
Ltd, London, 1980.

## DEPARTMENT OF EMPLOYMENT LEAFLETS

The Department of Employment issues regularly updated
leaflets which cover employment law on an easy-to-read
basis and which can be helpful, in the first instance, to
assist you in deciding whether you can take a complaint
further. These leaflets are obtainable at Jobcentres, Law
Centres, CABx, DSS Offices.

*Leaflet number:*
1 Written statement of main terms and conditions of
 employment.
2 Redundancy consultation and notification.
3 Employee's rights on insolvency of employer.
4 Employment rights for the expectant mother.
5 Suspension on medical grounds under health and
 safety regulations.

6 Facing redundancy? — time off for job hunting or to arrange training.
7 PL 871. Union membership and non-union rights.
8 Itemised pay statements.
9 Guarantee payments.
10 Employment rights on the transfer of an undertaking.
11 Rules governing continuous employment.
12 Time off for public duties.
13 Unfairly dismissed?
14 Rights to notice and reasons for dismissal.
15 Union secret ballots.
16 Redundancy payments.
17 Limits on payments.

# SPECIMEN FORMS

## PENSION FORECAST FORM

**You can get a Pension Forecast if you are**

- a woman under 59 years 8 months or a man under 64 years 8 months

All you have to do is fill in the attached form and send it to us at

RPFA Unit
Room 37D
Newcastle Upon Tyne NE98 1YX

**What your pension forecast will show**

**Basic Pension**

This is the part of your State Retirement Pension that depends on the National Insurance you pay in the time you would normally be working.

**Your forecast will tell you**

1 the amount of Basic Pension in today's money that you can expect to get based on the National Insurance you have already paid.

2 the amount of Basic Pension in today's money that you can expect to get based on the National Insurance you have already paid and any future National Insurance you are likely to pay.

3 what, if anything, you can do to get a better Basic Pension.

**Additional Pension and contracted-out deductions**

Additional Pension is the part of your pension that depends on your earnings since April 1978.
A contracted-out deduction is paid by your employer's contracted-out occupational pension scheme. It is the least amount of occupational pension that you must be paid and you get instead of all, or part of, your Additional Pension.

**Your forecast will tell you, in today's money**

4 the amount of Additional Pension, taking account of any contracted-out deduction, that you can expect to get based on the National Insurance you have already paid.

5 the amount of Additional Pension, taking account of any contracted-out deduction, you can expect to get if your earnings go up at the same rate as inflation.

6 the amount of Additional Pension, taking account of any contracted-out deduction, you can expect to get if your earnings go up at 1.5% more than the rate of inflation

BR19

147

# SPECIMEN FORMS

## 2. Marital status

**Have you ever had a different surname?**
**This might have been your maiden name.**

No ☐
Yes ☐   What was your surname? [_____]

3. **We need to know about your marital status. This is because your Retirement Pension may be affected by a spouse's National Insurance (NI) contributions.** We use spouse to mean your wife or your husband. Please tick the description that applies to you, and answer the questions.

☐ **Married**
What is your date of marriage? [  /  /  ]

☐ **Married but about to get divorced**
What is the expected date of the divorce? [  /  /  ]

☐ **Divorced**
What was the date of the divorce? [  /  /  ]

☐ **Widowed**
What date were you widowed on? [  /  /  ]
Are you getting any Widowed Mother's Allowance or Widow's Pension?

No ☐
Yes ☐  What is your reference number.
It is on the front of your order book or on the letter that we sent you about getting your benefit paid direct into an account.

Numbers [ ][ ][ ][ ][ ][ ]  Letters [ ][ ]

☐ **Single.**

4. **Have you ticked married but about to get divorced or divorced or widowed?**

No ☐
Yes ☐  **Please tell us about your marriage.**
If you have been married more than once, only tell us about your last spouse here.

**The date of your marriage** [  /  /  ]

**Your spouse's full name** [_____]

**Your spouse's date of birth** [  /  /  ]

**Your spouse's National Insurance (NI) number**
Letters [ ][ ]  Numbers [ ][ ][ ][ ][ ][ ]  Letter [ ]

**Your spouse's last address, if it is different to the address you have written at the beginning of this form.** [_____]

5. **Were you widowed before April 1978?**
**You only need to answer this question if you are a woman**

No ☐
Yes ☐  **Have you remarried since then?**
No ☐
Yes ☐  **Please tell us**
**The date you were widowed** [  /  /  ]
**The date you married your late husband** [  /  /  ]
**The date you remarried** [  /  /  ]

6. We need to know what you are doing now.
Please tick any of these descriptions that
apply to you.

☐ Working for an employer

☐ Self-employed

☐ Not working

☐ Signing on as unemployed

### 7. About National Insurance

We need to know what National
Insurance (NI) contributions you are
paying at the moment. Please tick the
descriptions that apply to you.

☐ Paying full-rate NI contributions

☐ Paying reduced-rate
NI contributions

☐ Paying voluntary NI contributions

☐ Not paying any NI contributions

### 8. About benefits

We need to know if you are getting any of
the benefits listed here. Please tick any
that you are getting.

☐ Dependant's War Pension (sometimes called War Widow's Pension)

☐ Industrial Death Benefit

☐ Statutory Sick Pay (SSP)

☐ Invalidity Benefit

☐ Severe Disablement Allowance

☐ Invalid Care Allowance

☐ Job Release Allowance

☐ Unemployment Benefit

☐ Child Benefit

What is the date of birth of your
youngest child or only child?  [ / / ]

What is the date of birth of your
oldest child if you have more than
one?  [ / / ]

If you get your Child Benefit paid by
order book, is your name above the
main address on the cover of the
book?

No ☐

Yes ☐

If you get your Child Benefit paid into
a bank or building society account, is
your own name and address shown
on the letter about Child Benefit we
send you once a year?

No ☐

Yes ☐

### 9. Living abroad

Have you ever lived outside England,
Scotland and Wales since you were 16?

No ☐

Yes ☐   Where did you live? [                    ]

# SPECIMEN FORMS

---

**10. Extra information**

- Your Pension Forecast will tell you
  - how much Retirement Pension you are already entitled to
  - how much Retirement Pension you will be entitled to when you are 60 (for a woman) or 65 (for a man) if you pay NI contributions until then.

- We can also tell you what may happen to your Retirement Pension in different situations. If you want us to include extra information in your forecast, please tick the things you want to know about.

☐ What if I go on working after I am 60 (for a woman) or 65 (for a man)? Tell us the date you may go on working till ___/___/___

☐ What if I stop working before I am 60 (for a woman) or 65 (for a man)? Tell us the date you may stop working. ___/___/___

☐ What if I go abroad? Tell us the country that you might go to. _____

☐ What if I stop paying reduced-rate NI, and start paying full-rate NI? Tell us the date when you might change ___/___/___ Tell us what your anual earnings are now £_____

☐ What if my marital status changes? Please tell us what you think your marital status might change to

☐ Married on ___/___/___
☐ Divorced on ___/___/___
☐ Widowed

☐ What if I pay the NI that I have not paid in the past?

☐ What if my annual earnings change? Tell us what they might change to, or the % that they might go up. _____

**Signature** _____

**Date** ___/___/___

---

**11. What to do now**

1. Check that you have answered all the questions that apply to you

2. Send the form to us at

   RPFA Unit
   Room 37D
   Central Office
   Newcastle upon Tyne
   NE98 1YX

Printed in the U.K. for H.M.S.O. 9/88 Dd 8151202 C 750 38806 019*8

**Form to apply for**

**A Pension Forecast**

| | Letters | Numbers | | Letter |
|---|---|---|---|---|
| Your National Insurance (NI) number | | | | |

Your surname

Your other names

Your title — Mr/Mrs/Miss/Ms

Your date of birth — /    /

Your address

Post code

| | Code | Number |
|---|---|---|
| Your daytime phone number | | |

SPECIMEN FORMS

**Graduated Retirement Benefit**

This is based on the amount of graduated National Insurance you have paid.

**Your forecast will tell you**

7 how many units of Graduated Retirement you have and what they are worth at today's rates

**If you are widowed or divorced**

Your late or former spouse's National Insurance can sometimes be used to help you get a better pension.

**Your forecast will tell you**

8 the amount of pension, including Basic Pension, Additional Pension, Contracted-out deduction, and Graduated Retirement Benefit, that you can expect to get using your late or former spouse's National Insurance.

# SELF-CERTIFICATE FORM FOR SICKNESS AND INVALIDITY

---

## Self-certificate

And Sickness and Invalidity Benefit claim form

# SC1

### KEEP THESE NOTES

---

#### Statutory sick pay

- Only employed people can get Statutory Sick Pay (SSP).
  You can use this form for SSP if your employer wishes.

- To get SSP you must be sick for at least 4 days in a row counting Saturdays and Sundays.

- For SSP you only need to fill in sections 1-5 and send this form to your employer.

- There is more about SSP in leaflet NI244 available from your local Social Security office.

---

#### Sickness benefit and Invalidity benefit

- Employees can only get these benefits if they are not covered by SSP. You must claim on form SSP 1 (E) or SSP 1 (T) issued by your employer.

- You can only get benefit if you are sick for at least 4 days in a row counting Saturdays but not Sundays.
  (Patients getting dialysis, radiotherapy, chemotherapy or plasmapheresis treatment should look at leaflet NI16, as different rules apply to them.)

- **If you are sick for 4, 5 or 6 days** in a row counting Saturdays but not Sundays wait until your last day of sickness and then fill in this form.

- **If you know you will be sick for more than 6 days** counting Saturdays but not Sundays fill in this form now.

- When you have filled in this form, send it at once to your local Social Security office. There are time limits for claiming and any delay can lose you benefit. Details are set out in leaflet NI16 (available from your local Social Security office).

- **If you are still sick after 6 days** ask your doctor for a sick note. Doctors do not have to issue sick notes for the first week of sickness but don't delay seeing your doctor if you need medical advice.

Please turn over the page

Form SC1 (1988)

- There is more about Sickness Benefit in leaflet NI16, and more about Invalidity Benefit in leaflet NI16A – available from your local Social Security Office.

# OTHER HELP YOU MAY GET

- Attendance Allowance – You may get this if you're severely disabled and also require a lot of looking after for at least six months. See leaflet NI205.

- Industrial Injuries Disablement Benefit – You may get this if you become disabled as the result of either an accident at work or one of the prescribed industrial diseases. See leaflet NI6.

- Mobility Allowance – You may get this if you're unable, or virtually unable to walk because of your physical disablement. See leaflet NI211.

- Income Support – If you can't manage on the money you have coming in you may be able to get Income Support. Leaflet SB1 is available from your local Social Security or Post Office.

- Help with fares to and from Hospital – You may get this if you're claiming Income Support or living on a low income. See leaflet H11.

- Help with rent and rates – You may be able to get help whether or not you're working. It depends on your income, the rent and rates you pay and the size of your family. Ask at your local council offices for a Housing Benefit claim form.

- Help for disabled people – There is a wide range of services and benefits for disabled people. See leaflet HB1.

- Further Benefits – If you're living on a low income you may be able to get some of the following additional benefits. You qualify automatically for them if you get Income Support or Family Credit.

    Free NHS dental treatment (see leaflet D.11)
    Free NHS voucher to help with cost of glasses (see leaflet G11)
    Free NHS prescriptions (see leaflet P11)
    Free hospital appliances (ask at the hospital).

- Prescription Season Tickets – If you don't qualify for free prescriptions and need a lot of things on prescription, you may save money by buying a pre-payment 'season ticket'. Get Form FP95 (in Scotland form EC95) – also from Post Offices.

# Self-certificate

## And Sickness and Invalidity Benefit claim form

# SC1

**1** | About you

**PLEASE USE BLOCK LETTERS**
If you cannot fill this form in yourself, ask someone else to do so and to
sign it for you

| Surname: Mr/Mrs/Miss/Ms |
| First names |
| Present address |
| Postcode |

Date of birth

National Insurance number

CLOCK/STAFF/WORKS NUMBER

**2** | Details of sickness

Give details of your sickness. Words like
'illness' or 'unwell' are not enough

Please say briefly why you are unfit for work

- Is your sickness due to an accident which happened while you were
working for an employer?

Tick one box          YES ☐          NO ☐

- Is your sickness due to a prescribed industrial disease caused by
conditions at work, while you were working for an employer?

Tick one box          YES ☐          NO ☐

NOTE: This does not apply if the accident or prescribed disease
occurred while you were self-employed.

FORM SC1 (1988)

**3** Period of sickness

If you do not fill in this section or if you fill it in wrongly, any payment of benefit due to you may be delayed.

| | | |
|---|---|---|
| **Everyone to fill in** | Date you became unfit for work | day ___ ___ ___ 19 |
| Do not complete if you are unemployed | Date you last worked | day ___ ___ ___ 19 |
| | Time you finished work | time ___ am/pm |
| **Night shift workers only** | When did your last shift begin? | time ___ am/pm   day ___ ___ ___ 19 |
| **Everyone to fill in** | Do you expect to be unfit for work for more than 7 days? YES ☐ NO ☐<br>If you ticked 'YES', go to part 5 | |

**4** Returning to work

date month year

| | |
|---|---|
| Last day of sickness before starting or seeking work | day ___ ___ ___ 19 |
| Date you intend to start or seek work | day ___ ___ ___ 19 |

**Night shift workers only** Shift will begin at time ___ am/pm and end next day at time ___ am/pm

**5** If you are claiming Sickness or Invalidity Benefit

Go to part 6 'Your work' — do not sign below

If you are using this form for Statutory Sick Pay

Stop here. Sign below, and send this form to your employer

Signature        Date

Remember, if you are sick for a second week, your employer may want a sick note.

**6** Your work      Are you?:–

**Tick one or more boxes**

Employed ☐    Unemployed ☐    A student ☐

Self employed ☐    Other ☐

What is your usual job?

Please turn over the page

## 7 Your employer and SSP

Before your present illness began, have you in the last 8 weeks been off work sick for at least 4 days in a row?

Tick one box          YES ☐   NO ☐

If you ticked 'YES', please give the name and address of the employer you were working for.

| |
|---|
| |

## 8 Your doctor

Doctor's name and address

| |
|---|
| |

## 9 In hospital

Tick one box

Have you been a hospital in-patient since you became unfit for work?          YES ☐ NO ☐

If you ticked 'YES', please state the name and address of the hospital

| |
|---|
| |

## 10 You and your family

**Phone number** where we can ring you during the day [ ]

Tick one box

Are you?   single ☐   married ☐   widowed ☐   divorced ☐

You can claim extra benefit for your spouse or a person looking after children.

- **A SEPARATE CLAIM MUST BE MADE.** If you want a claim form sent to you, tick the box or boxes below:–

SPOUSE ☐,   PERSON LOOKING AFTER CHILDREN ☐,

CHILDREN ☐ (see the '**NOTE**' below).

NOTE:  You can only claim extra money for children if you are a man over 65 or a woman over 60 or if you are claiming Invalidity Benefit.

## 11 Other benefits

- **Tick any benefits that you are getting or that you have already claimed.**

Tick one or more boxes

| Income Support ☐ | Unemployability Supplement ☐ |
| War Widow's Pension ☐ | Job Release Allowance ☐ |
| Youth Training Scheme Allowance ☐ | Invalid Care Allowance ☐ |
| Enterprise Allowance ☐ | |

- **Are you getting any other Social Security benefit, pension or allowance or waiting to hear the result of a claim for one.**

Tick one box

YES ☐ NO ☐

If YES, state which

- **Is anyone getting extra benefit for you as a dependant?** NOTE: Also tick 'YES' if they are waiting for the result of a claim for extra benefit.

Tick one box

YES ☐ NO ☐ If 'YES' please state:

His/her name

Address

Postcode

Name of benefit

- **Have you received any money for training or rehabilitation in the past 8 weeks?** YES ☐ NO ☐

Tick one box

If 'YES', where was it from?

---

## 12 Declaration

**Remember: if you knowingly give wrong or false information you may be prosecuted.**

**I declare** that I have not worked during the period of sickness which I have stated and that the information given is correct and complete.

I claim benefit

**I agree** to my doctor giving medical information relevant to my claim to a doctor in the Regional Medical Service

Signature                                    Date

If you have signed on behalf of the person claiming, tick the box ☐

---

**Send the form immediately to your local Social Security office to avoid losing any benefit**

Printed in the U.K. for H.M.S.O. 10/87 Dd 8104489 C 120000 38806 G1427

# APPLICATION TO AN INDUSTRIAL TRIBUNAL

# Application to an Industrial Tribunal

**Please read the notes opposite before filling in this form.**

**1** Say what type of complaint(s) you want the tribunal to decide *(see note opposite).*

**2** Give your name and address etc. in CAPITALS *(see note opposite).*

Mr/Mrs
Miss/Ms

Address

Telephone

Date of birth

**3** Please give the name and address of your representative, if you have one.

Name

Address

Telephone

**4** Give the name and address of the employer, person or body (the respondent) you are complaining about *(see note opposite).*

Name

Address

Telephone

Give the place where you worked or applied for work, if different from above.

Name

Address

Telephone

**5** Please say what job you did for the employer (or what job you applied for). If this does not apply, please say what your connection was with the employer.

**IT 1 and IT 1(Scot) (Revised July 1987)**

**Please continue overleaf**

**6** Please give the number of normal basic hours you worked per week.

Hours [          ] per week

**7** Basic wage / salary £ [          ] per [     ]

Average take home pay £ [          ] per [     ]

Other bonuses / benefits £ [          ] per [     ]

**8** Please give the dates of your employment *(if applicable)*

Began on [          ]

Ended on [          ]

**9** If your complaint is **not** about dismissal, please give the date when the action you are complaining about took place (or the date when you first knew about it).

Date [          ]

**10** Give the full details of your complaint *(see note opposite)*.

**11 Unfair dismissal claimants only** (Please tick a box to show what you would want if you win your case).

[ ] Reinstatement: to carry on working in your old job as before

[ ] Re-engagement: to start another job, or a new contract, with your old employer
Orders for reinstatement or re-engagement normally include an award of compensation for loss of earnings.

[ ] Compensation only: to get an award of money
You can change your mind later. The Tribunal will take your preference into account, but will not be bound by it.

Signature:                                           Date:

# COUNTY COURT FORM REQUESTING ISSUE OF DEFAULT SUMMONS (N201)

## Form for requesting issue of a default summons

- Please read the notes over the page before filling in this form. You will also find it useful to read the booklet "Small Claims in the County Court" which is available from any county court office.

**For court use**

| Case number: | |

Summons in form    N1 ☐
                       N2 ☐

Service by:       Post ☐
            Plaintiff('s Solr) ☐

**1 Plaintiff's**
(Person making the claim)
Full name
Address

- Please be careful when filling in the request form.
- Type or write in block capitals using **black ink.**
- If the details of claim are on a separate sheet you must give the court a copy for its own use and a copy for each defendant.
- You can get help to complete this form at any county court office or citizens' advice bureau.

**2 Plaintiff's solicitor Address**

Ref/tel no.

**3 Defendant's**
(Person against whom the claim is made)
Name
Address

**4 What the claim is for**
Give brief description of type of claim.

**5** If the defendant does not live within the district of the court, the plaintiff states that the cause of action arose:

**6 Particulars of the plaintiff's claim**

**7** 
| Plaintiff's claim | |
| Court fee | |
| Solicitor's costs | |
| **Total Amount** | |

For court use     Issued on

## Small Claims Procedure

- Any defended claim for £500 of less will be automatically dealt with by arbitration. If you do not want the claim to be dealt with by arbitration you will have to apply to the court. The court office can give you more details.

**9** If the claim exceeds £500 and you would like it to be dealt with by arbitration please tick the box below.

The claim exceeds £500 and I would like it to be dealt with by arbitration ☐

**8 Signed**
Plaintiff('s solicitor)
(or see attached form "Particulars of claim")

N 201    Request for default summons

Printed in the UK for HMSO. D.8035033 2,000m 10/86.

# SPECIMEN FORMS

## Notes

### 1 Plaintiff
Enter the plaintiff's full name and address or place of business.
If the plaintiff is:
- a company registered under the Companies Act, 1985, give the address of the registered office and describe it as such.
- a person trading in a name other than his own, give his own name followed by the words "trading as" and the name which he trades under.
- two or more co-partners suing in the name of their firm, add "A Firm".
- an assignee, say so and give the name, address and occupation of assignor.
- a minor required to sue by next friend, write down the fact, and give the full names, address or place of business, and occupation of next friend.
- suing in a representative capacity, say in what capacity.

### 2 Plaintiff's solicitor
If the summons is entered by a solicitor the name, address and reference number should be put in this space. This space may also be used for address of legal departments etc.

### 3 Defendant
Enter the defendant's surname, and (where known) his or her initials or names in full. Also give the defendant's address or place of business (if an owner of the business). Say if male or female and if under 18 state "minor".
If the defendant is:
- a company registered under the Companies Act, 1985, the address given must be the registered office of the company, and must be described as such.
- a person trading in a name other than his own who is sued under such name, add "A Trading Name".
- two or more co-partners sued in the name of their firm, add "Firm".
- sued in a representative capacity, say in what capacity.

### 4 What the claim is for
Put a brief description of your dispute in the box (e.g. price of goods sold and delivered, work done, money due under an agreement).

### 5 Jurisdiction
If the defendant or one of the defendants does not live or carry on business within the district of the court you must show that the cause of action (i.e. the circumstances of the transaction giving rise to the claim) arose wholly or partly within the district of the court. The court can deal with the action, if, for instance, the claim is founded on:
- a contract made at an address within the district,
- a contract under which payment is to be made at an address within the district,
- an accident which happened within the district.
If any of these apply you must enter the address in the box. The defendant is entitled to apply to the court to have the case transferred to his local court.

### 6 Particulars of the plaintiff's claim
Give a brief statement of the facts of your claim and the amount for which you are suing. Include any relevant dates and sufficient details to inform the defendant of the nature of your claim against him. He is entitled to ask for further details. If there is not enough space or the details of your claim are too complicated you should attach a separate sheet to each copy of the summons. You can obtain forms of particulars of claim from any county court office.

### 7 Amount claimed
Enter the total amount you are claiming. The court fee and solicitors costs are based on this and you should enter these too. A leaflet setting out the current fee is available from the court.

### 8 Signature
The person filling in the form should sign and date it unless attaching details of claim, in which case, the attached sheets should be signed.

### 9 Claims exceeding £500
If your claim exceeds £500 you can ask for it to be dealt with by arbitration. Solicitors costs and grounds for setting aside an arbitrator's award are strictly limited.

To be completed by the court

Served on:

By posting on:

Officer:

# INDEX

Page numbers in *italics* refer to tables/flow charts.

ACAS, 17, 78; how they can help, 135
acceptance of job, 7
Acts of Parliament, 30–31
addresses, 141–144
advice, 107
Advisory, Conciliation, Arbitration Service *see* ACAS
Agricultural Wages Board, 18
alternative employment, 97–98
animals, 113
antenatal care, 50, 112–113
appeals, against decision of Tribunal, 140

bank holidays, 9, 10
bankruptcy, 99–101

capability, 72–74; sickness, 80–81
chemicals, 113
claim, Industrial Tribunal, 132–135
claim, making a, 35–36
compensation, 134
conditions, 1
consideration of a job, 7
constructive dismissal, 85–87
consultation, 95
contract of employment: *5*; disappears by law, 21–22; employed, 2; expiry of fixed term, 21; self-employed, 3; serious change in, 69–70; terms of, 4–6, *19*; verbal agreement, 1; way it works, 6; written terms, 1
contractual maternity pay, 121
contractual notice, 24–26
contractual sick pay, 11–12
costs and expenses, Industrial Tribunal, 139
counter-notice, 106–107
custom and practice, 18, 19

Department of Employment, 31, 99; leaflets, 145–146
disabled employees, 44

disciplinary procedure, 16–18, 55–56
discrimination, 37–43
dismissal: 16, *88*; date of, 71–72; fair, 72–77; misconduct, 74–75; pregnancy, 114–115; prevented in law from working, 75; rights, 61–63; summary, 22; trade union activities, 82–84; unfair, 77–86; without notice, 27

employee, death of, 101
employer, closes his business, 99–101
employer, death of, 101
employment: after working for one month, 53–54; after working 13 weeks, 54–56; after working 26 weeks, 56–57; rights, 49–53
Employment Appeal Tribunal, 140
Employment Protection (Consolidation) Act, 31–33, 48, 59, 71, 89, 104
Equal Opportunities Commission, 33
equal pay, 52–53
Equal Pay Act, 33–37
equivalently rated work, 34–35
expressed terms, 4

fair dismissal, pregnancy, 114–115
fixed-term contract, 21, 84–85
forms, specimen, 147–149

grievance procedure, 15–16, 55, 131–132
gross misconduct, 18
guarantee payments, 64–65, 107–110

hazards at work when pregnant, 113–114
Health and Safety at Work Act, 43–45
Health and Safety Executive, 45
hiving down, 67
holiday entitlement, 9–10
hours, reduction in, 116–117

hours, 9
Hungary, 111

illness when pregnant, 113
implied terms, 4–5
imposed terms, 6
Industrial Tribunals: 32, 127–135, 136–140; decision, 137–139, *138*; qualifying for claims, 59–61, *60*; what happens at, 136–137; who sits on, 136
interviews, questions to ask at, 8–18

job-hunting, 51

lay-off, 63–64, 102–103
lay-off notice, *108*
legal aid, Tribunals, 128–129
'like' work, 34

maternity allowance, 125–126
maternity leave, 120–126; refusal to give job back, 81–82
maternity rights, 65
miscarriages, 125
misconduct, 74–75, 77–78; gross, 78–80
money in lieu, 26–27, 95

notice: 22–28; arrangements, 10; employer, 28; entitlement, *25*; not required to work, 27

occupational pension, 13–14
offer of job, 7
overtime, 9

pay statement, 49–50
payments during maternity leave, 121–125
pension, 12–15
personal pensions, 14
point of law appeal, 140
pregnancy, 44–45, 111–120
premature birth, 124
public duties, 50

qualification, 72–74
questions at interview, 8–18

Race Relations Act, 39–43
Race Relations Act, exceptions, 42
racial discrimination, 52
racial segregation, 41

redundancy: 51, 89–101; fund, 99; payments; how to claim, 105–106; result of lay-off, 104–107; right to payment, 63; unfair, 82
relationship, between employer/ employee, 2
retirement, leaving before, 15
returning to work, 117–120
rights, 49–53

sale of business, 65–67
selection for redundancy, 93–94
self-employed, 3
self-employed, pensions, 14–15
sex discrimination, 52; pregnancy, 115–116
Sex Discrimination Act, 37–39
short-time notice, *108*
short-time working, 63–64, 104
sick-pay, 10–12
social security appeals tribunal (SATT), 29
specimen forms, 147–149
state benefits, 28
state earnings related pension (SERPs), 13
statutory maternity pay, 121–125
statutory notice, 23
statutory redundancy payment, 90
statutory rights, *58*
statutory sick pay (SSP), 10–11
stillbirth, 125

takeovers, 65–67
termination, 21–22; by agreement, 21; by breach, 22
time limits for claim, 31, 105; Tribunals, 129–131, *130*
time off, 50–52, 95–97
trade union activities, 82–84
Trade Union and Labour Relations Act, 45–46
Trade Union Law, 45–46
Transfer of Undertakings Regulations, 65
transfers, 67–69, 98–99
twins, 125

unemployment benefits, 28–29; disallowed, 29
unfair dismissal: 77–86; pregnancy, 115
union duties, 51–52

VDUs, 113–114
verbal contract, 1

verbal notice, 23
victimisation, 38, 41

wages, 8
Wages Act, 46–47

Wages Councils, 18
warnings, 17
week in hand, 8–9
work of equal value, 35
working out notice, 26

All Optima books are available at your bookshop or newsagent, or can be ordered from the following address:

Optima, Cash Sales Department,
PO Box 11, Falmouth, Cornwall TR10 9EN

Please send cheque or postal order (no currency), and allow 60p for postage and packing for the first book, plus 25p for the second book and 15p for each additional book ordered up to a maximum charge of £1.90 in the UK.

Customers in Eire and BFPO please allow 60p for the first book, 25p for the second book plus 15p per copy for the next 7 books, thereafter 9p per book.

Overseas customers please allow £1.25 for postage and packing for the first book and 28p per copy for each additional book.